DOG TRAINING GUIDE

A Complete Handbook for Obedience, Behaviour Correction, and Advanced Canine Training

DR. SAMANTHA J. HURD

Copyright © 2025 by Dr. Samantha J. Hurd. All rights reserved.

No part of this book may be reproduced, stored in a retrieval system, or transmitted in any form or by any means—electronic, mechanical, photocopying, recording, or otherwise—without the prior written permission of the author or publisher, except in the case of brief quotations embodied in critical reviews and certain other noncommercial uses permitted by copyright law.

Table of Content

INTRODUCTION — 7

The Psychology of Dogs: How They Learn and Respond — 7
Building Trust and Strengthening the Bond Through Training — 7
Common Training Myths and Misconceptions — 8
Why Every Dog Needs Training—Regardless of Size, Breed, or Temperament — 9
Choosing the Right Training Approach — 9
Clicker Training — 9
The Journey Ahead: What to Expect from This Book — 10

CHAPTER 1: PREPARING FOR TRAINING SUCCESS — 11

Choosing the Right Training Method for Your Dog — 11
Understanding Your Dog's Breed, Temperament, and Natural Instincts — 16
Creating a Positive Training Environment — 19
Essential Training Tools and Equipment — 23
Establishing Leadership: Becoming a Confident Pack Leader — 27

CHAPTER 2: PUPPY TRAINING FOUNDATIONS — 31

The Critical Socialization Period: What to Do and What to Avoid — 31
Basic Puppy Obedience: Teaching Name Recognition, Sit, Stay, and Come — 34
Crate Training and Housebreaking: Effective Potty Training Methods — 37
Preventing and Correcting Biting, Chewing, and Destructive Behavior — 41
When to Seek Professional Help — 43
Leash Training for Young Puppies — 44

CHAPTER 3: BASIC OBEDIENCE TRAINING — 47

Teaching Essential Commands: Sit, Stay, Down, Come, and Leave It — 47
Positive Reinforcement vs. Corrections: Finding the Right Balance — 50
Understanding Corrections in Training — 52
Finding the Right Balance — 52
Using Treats, Toys, and Praise Effectively — 53
Using Treats in Training — 54
Using Toys as Rewards — 55
Using Praise Effectively — 56
Combining Treats, Toys, and Praise for Maximum Effect — 56
Common Mistakes to Avoid — 56
Overcoming Common Training Challenges — 57

CHAPTER 4: LEASH TRAINING AND OFF-LEASH CONTROL — 62

Choosing the Right Leash, Collar, or Harness for Training	62
Teaching Loose Leash Walking and Preventing Pulling	67
Essential Tools for Loose Leash Walking	68
Step-by-Step Guide to Teaching Loose Leash Walking	68
Additional Tips for Preventing Pulling	70
Correcting Lunging, Jumping, and Leash Reactivity	71
Off-Leash Training: Building Trust and Control in Open Spaces	75
Training Reliable Recall: Getting Your Dog to Come Every Time	79

CHAPTER 5: BEHAVIORAL TRAINING AND PROBLEM-SOLVING — 84

Key Factors That Influence Behavior:	84
How to Stop Excessive Barking	87
When to Seek Professional Help	91
Dealing with Aggression: Causes and Solutions	91
Causes of Aggression	92
Solutions for Managing Aggression	93
Preventing Aggressive Behavior	94
Separation Anxiety: Prevention and Treatment	95
Destructive Chewing and Resource Guarding	99
Fear and Anxiety in Dogs: Signs, Causes, and Management	103
Socialization with People, Dogs, and Other Pets	106

CHAPTER 6: ADVANCED OBEDIENCE AND SPECIALIZED TRAINING — 110

Training for Longer Stays, Distance Commands, and Hand Signals	110
Clicker Training: How It Works and Step-by-Step Guide	113
Step-by-Step Guide to Clicker Training	114
Using Whistle, Vibrations, and Other Alternative Training Methods	116
Teaching Fun Tricks: Roll Over, Shake Hands, Play Dead, and More	120
Scent Work, Fetch, and Agility Training	123

CHAPTER 7: TRAINING FOR THERAPY AND SERVICE DOGS — 128

The Difference Between Therapy, Service, and Emotional Support Dogs	128
Key Differences Between Service Dogs, Therapy Dogs, and Emotional Support Dogs	131
Public Behavior and Socialization for Assistance Dogs	135
Socialization for Assistance Dogs	136
Preparing for Therapy and Service Dog Certification	139

CHAPTER 8: CORRECTING BAD HABITS AND UNWANTED BEHAVIORS — 144

Jumping on People: Causes and Solutions	144
Risks and Problems Associated with Jumping	145
Effective Solutions for Preventing and Correcting Jumping	145

Digging, Counter-Surfing, and Stealing Food	148
Chasing Cars, Bikes, or Other Animals	151
Overexcitement, Hyperactivity, and Impulse Control in Dogs	155

CHAPTER 9: TRAINING FOR SPECIFIC BREEDS AND TEMPERAMENTS — 160

How Training Differs for Different Dog Breeds	160
High-Energy vs. Low-Energy Dogs: Adapting Your Methods	164
Training Low-Energy Dogs	166
Training Stubborn, Independent, or Hard-to-Train Breeds	168
Overcoming Common Training Challenges	170
How to Work with Rescue and Shelter Dogs	172
Building Trust and Establishing a Connection	172
Helping Rescue Dogs Adjust to a New Home	174
Working with Professional Trainers and Behaviorists	175

CHAPTER 10: TRAINING FOR SPECIAL NEEDS AND SENIOR DOGS — 176

Deaf Dog Training: Communicating Without Sound	176
Signs That a Dog May Be Deaf	176
Training Methods for Deaf Dogs	177
Preventing Startle Reactions	178
Building Confidence and Strengthening the Bond	179
Blind Dog Training: Helping Dogs Navigate the World	179
Signs That a Dog May Be Blind	180
Training Methods for Blind Dogs	180
Preventing Startle Reactions	181
Building Confidence and Strengthening the Bond	182
Training Senior Dogs: Adjusting Methods for Older Canines	182
Continuing Socialization for Senior Dogs	185
The Importance of Exercise and Enrichment	185
Strengthening the Bond with an Older Dog	186
Working with Dogs with Physical Disabilities	186

CHAPTER 11: SEASONAL AND OUTDOOR TRAINING CHALLENGES — 191

Training in Cold Weather and Snow	191
Alternative Indoor Training for Extremely Cold Weather	194
Cold Weather Safety Tips for Outdoor Training	194
Keeping Training Fun in Hot and Humid Conditions	195
Training in Crowded or Noisy Environments	199
Safety Considerations for Outdoor Adventures	203

CHAPTER 12: MAINTAINING GOOD BEHAVIOR FOR LIFE — 208

Reinforcing Training Over Time	208
Preventing Behavioral Regression	211
How to Keep Training Fun and Engaging for Your Dog	211
Common Mistakes Owners Make and How to Avoid Them	213
Creating a Customized Training Plan for Your Dog	217

FINAL THOUGHTS   221

Introduction

Understanding the Importance of Proper Dog Training

Dogs have been by our side for thousands of years, evolving from wild wolves to loyal companions, protectors, and working animals. They are often referred to as "man's best friend," and for good reason—dogs provide companionship, love, and unwavering loyalty. However, a well-behaved dog doesn't come automatically; it is the result of proper training, socialization, and guidance from a responsible owner.

Dog training is not just about teaching tricks or controlling behavior; it is a fundamental part of responsible dog ownership. A well-trained dog is not only happier but also safer, healthier, and more integrated into family life. Training helps prevent problem behaviors, reduces stress for both the dog and owner, and fosters a relationship built on trust and mutual understanding.

The Psychology of Dogs: How They Learn and Respond

Understanding how dogs think and learn is the foundation of successful training. Dogs are not humans; they perceive the world differently and communicate primarily through body language, vocalizations, and environmental cues. Unlike humans, who rely heavily on verbal communication, dogs are highly attuned to non-verbal signals, consistency, and reinforcement.

Dogs learn primarily through association and reinforcement. If a behavior results in a positive outcome (such as a treat, praise, or playtime), they are more likely to repeat it. If a behavior leads to an unpleasant outcome (such as being ignored or a firm correction), they are less likely to repeat it. This is why training methods based on positive reinforcement—rewarding good behavior—are highly effective and humane.

One of the biggest mistakes dog owners make is assuming that dogs think like humans. While dogs are incredibly intelligent, they do not understand human emotions in the same way we do. Instead, they rely on consistency, routine, and clear signals from their owners to interpret what is expected of them.

Building Trust and Strengthening the Bond Through Training

Training is not just about obedience—it is about building a lifelong bond with your dog. The most successful training occurs when a dog feels safe, respected, and connected to its owner. Training provides an opportunity to establish clear communication, develop mutual respect, and create a structure that makes dogs feel secure.

Dogs are pack animals by nature, and in a domestic setting, they look to their human family for leadership. When owners provide clear, consistent guidance, dogs feel more confident and secure. An untrained dog, on the other hand, may experience confusion, anxiety, and behavioral issues due to the lack of clear structure.

A strong bond between a dog and its owner is based on:

- Trust – Your dog should trust that you will provide for its needs and keep it safe.
- Consistency – Dogs thrive on routine and clear expectations.
- Positive Reinforcement – Encouraging good behavior rather than focusing on punishment.
- Patience – Every dog learns at its own pace, and training should be approached with understanding and patience.

Common Training Myths and Misconceptions

There is a lot of misinformation about dog training, some of which has led to outdated or ineffective training techniques. Here are some common myths that need to be debunked:

Myth 1: "Old Dogs Can't Learn New Tricks"

Many people believe that once a dog reaches adulthood, it is too late to train them. This is false. While puppies may learn faster, adult and even senior dogs are fully capable of learning new behaviors and commands. The key is patience, consistency, and positive reinforcement.

Myth 2: "Dogs Should Be Dominated to Obey"

The outdated "dominance theory" suggests that dogs need to be dominated or physically corrected to obey. However, modern behavioral science has shown that positive reinforcement and leadership based on trust and respect are far more effective than forceful methods.

Myth 3: "Dogs Understand Human Speech Like We Do"

Dogs do not understand full sentences the way humans do. They rely on tone, body language, and repetitive association with specific words. This is why short, clear, and consistent commands work best in training.

Myth 4: "Some Breeds Are Untrainable"

While certain breeds may have different learning styles, every dog is trainable. Some breeds, such as working or herding dogs, may require more mental stimulation, while independent breeds may need extra motivation. With the right approach, every dog can learn obedience and good behavior.

Myth 5: "Punishment Is Necessary for Training"

Punishment-based methods can cause fear, anxiety, and aggression in dogs. Instead of punishing bad behavior, trainers should focus on redirecting behavior and rewarding positive actions.

Why Every Dog Needs Training—Regardless of Size, Breed, or Temperament

Many owners assume that only "problematic" dogs need training. In reality, all dogs benefit from proper training, regardless of their size, breed, or temperament. Even the most gentle and easygoing dogs need to learn basic commands and social skills.

Benefits of Training for Every Dog:

- Improves Safety – A trained dog is less likely to run into danger or engage in risky behaviors.
- Enhances Communication – Training helps dogs understand commands, leading to a smoother owner-dog relationship.
- Prevents Behavior Issues – Training prevents common issues like barking, chewing, jumping, and aggression.
- Encourages Mental Stimulation – Learning commands and tricks keeps dogs mentally engaged and happy.
- Strengthens Socialization – Well-trained dogs interact better with other dogs, people, and different environments.

Choosing the Right Training Approach

There is no one-size-fits-all approach to dog training, as different dogs respond to different methods. However, the most effective and humane training methods share the following principles:

Positive Reinforcement Training

This method rewards desired behaviors with treats, praise, or play. It is based on the principle that rewarded behaviors are repeated. Positive reinforcement has been scientifically proven to be the most effective and ethical training approach.

Clicker Training

Clicker training uses a small device that makes a clicking sound to mark the desired behavior, followed by a reward. This method helps dogs quickly associate specific actions with rewards.

Balanced Training

This approach combines positive reinforcement with gentle corrections when necessary. It is effective for training working dogs, service dogs, and dogs that need clear structure.

Force-Free Training

Force-free training focuses solely on rewards and redirection without any corrections or aversive tools. It is ideal for sensitive dogs that may become fearful with corrections.

The Journey Ahead: What to Expect from This Book

This book is designed to be the ultimate guide to dog training, covering everything from puppy socialization to advanced off-leash training. Whether you are a first-time dog owner or an experienced handler, this book will provide:

- Step-by-step training techniques for obedience, behavior correction, and fun tricks.
- Solutions to common behavioral problems, such as barking, aggression, separation anxiety, and leash pulling.
- Insights into breed-specific training, temperament differences, and training special needs dogs.
- Guidance on advanced training, including off-leash control, agility, and service dog preparation.

By the end of this book, you will have the knowledge and confidence to train your dog effectively, build a strong bond, and create a well-behaved, happy canine companion. Training is a journey, not a one-time event, and with patience, consistency, and the right techniques, every dog can become a well-mannered member of the family.

Now, let's begin this exciting journey into the world of dog training and behavior mastery!

Chapter 1: Preparing for Training Success

Successful dog training begins with the right approach. Understanding your dog's needs, choosing effective methods, and creating a positive environment lay the foundation for lifelong obedience and companionship.

Choosing the Right Training Method for Your Dog

Training a dog is both an art and a science. While all dogs have the capacity to learn, each dog is unique in temperament, intelligence, energy levels, and responsiveness to training. Choosing the right training method is essential to ensure effective learning, a positive experience for both the dog and the owner, and long-term behavioral success.

Understanding Your Dog's Individual Learning Style

Before selecting a training method, it is crucial to understand how your dog learns. Dogs process information differently based on their breed, age, personality, and previous experiences. Some dogs are naturally eager to please and quick to respond to commands, while others may be more independent or stubborn.

Key Factors That Affect a Dog's Learning Style:

1. Breed Characteristics – Some breeds, such as Border Collies and German Shepherds, are highly intelligent and quick learners, while others, like Afghan Hounds and Basenjis, may be more independent and require additional motivation.
2. Age and Development Stage – Puppies are more impressionable and absorb training quickly, while older dogs may need more patience and reinforcement. However, all dogs can learn regardless of age.
3. Temperament – Confident dogs may require firmer guidance, while shy or anxious dogs need a gentle, encouraging approach.
4. Energy Level – High-energy dogs may benefit from active, engaging training sessions, while lower-energy breeds might need shorter, more focused sessions.
5. Past Experiences – Rescue dogs or those with past trauma may require additional patience, trust-building, and a tailored training approach.

By considering these factors, owners can better determine which training method will be the most effective for their dog.

Popular Dog Training Methods

There are various training methodologies, each with its own philosophy and effectiveness depending on the dog's personality and the owner's goals. Below are the most widely used and scientifically supported dog training methods.

1. Positive Reinforcement Training

Positive reinforcement training is one of the most effective, humane, and scientifically backed methods of training. It involves rewarding desired behaviors with treats, praise, toys, or play, making it more likely that the dog will repeat those behaviors.

Key Principles:

- Reward behaviors you want to encourage.
- Ignore or redirect unwanted behaviors instead of punishing.
- Use consistent verbal cues and hand signals.
- Reinforce behaviors immediately after they occur to strengthen the association.

Best For:

- Puppies and adult dogs
- All breeds and temperaments
- Owners who prefer a humane and effective approach

Pros:

✔ Builds trust between dog and owner
✔ Encourages eager and enthusiastic learning
✔ Prevents fear and anxiety in dogs

Cons:

✘ Requires patience and consistency
✘ Some dogs may become overly reliant on treats (which can be mitigated by gradually transitioning to verbal praise)

2. Clicker Training

Clicker training is a subset of positive reinforcement training that uses a small device that makes a clicking sound to mark the precise moment a dog performs a desired behavior. The click is immediately followed by a reward, reinforcing the behavior.

Key Principles:

- The clicker serves as a clear, consistent marker for correct behavior.
- The dog learns that the sound of the click means a reward is coming.
- Reinforcement follows the behavior immediately for clarity.

Best For:

- Dogs that learn best with clear, consistent feedback
- Training complex behaviors and tricks
- Puppies and highly motivated dogs

Pros:

✔ Provides precise communication between trainer and dog
✔ Can be used for advanced training and behavioral shaping
✔ Works well for training deaf dogs when paired with hand signals

Cons:

✘ Requires owners to always have a clicker on hand
✘ Some dogs may take time to associate the clicker with rewards

3. Balanced Training (Positive Reinforcement with Corrections)

Balanced training combines positive reinforcement with fair corrections for undesired behavior. While positive reinforcement is used to encourage good behavior, corrections (such as a firm "No" or withholding a reward) help discourage unwanted behaviors.

Key Principles:

- Reward good behaviors to reinforce them.
- Correct undesired behaviors through non-harmful means, such as verbal cues, leash corrections, or removing rewards.
- Strive for a balance where the dog understands both what is expected and what is discouraged.

Best For:

- Dogs that require structure and clear expectations
- Owners comfortable with applying consistent discipline
- Working dogs, service dogs, or high-drive breeds

Pros:

✔ Provides a clear structure for the dog
✔ Can work effectively for more independent or stubborn breeds
✔ Helps maintain control in high-stimulation environments

Cons:

✘ If not used correctly, corrections can cause fear or confusion
✘ Requires experienced handling to ensure fairness and clarity

4. Relationship-Based Training

This method focuses on strengthening the bond between dog and owner through mutual trust, understanding, and respect. Instead of relying heavily on rewards or corrections, relationship-based training prioritizes clear communication and engagement.

Key Principles:

- Build a strong connection with your dog through interaction and trust.
- Use training sessions as opportunities to strengthen the bond.
- Keep training sessions fun and stress-free.

Best For:

- Owners looking to develop deep trust with their dog
- Dogs that respond well to personal engagement and interaction

Pros:

✔ Strengthens the emotional bond between dog and owner
✔ Creates an eager and motivated learner
✔ Encourages a calm and confident dog

Cons:

✗ May take longer to see results compared to structured methods
✗ Requires significant time and dedication

Choosing the Best Training Method for Your Dog

With multiple training methods available, selecting the right one depends on:

1. Your Dog's Personality – Energetic dogs may thrive with positive reinforcement and active training, while shy dogs may need gentle encouragement.
2. Your Training Goals – If you want basic obedience, positive reinforcement works well. If training for protection or service work, balanced training may be more suitable.
3. Your Experience Level – First-time dog owners may find positive reinforcement and clicker training easiest, while experienced handlers may use balanced training effectively.
4. Your Dog's Past Experiences – Rescue dogs with trauma may require relationship-based training to rebuild trust.

Common Mistakes When Choosing a Training Method

Many dog owners struggle with training due to mistakes in selecting or implementing training methods. Here are some common pitfalls to avoid:

- Inconsistency – Switching between methods too often confuses the dog.
- Using Harsh Punishments – This can lead to fear-based behaviors and anxiety.
- Lack of Patience – Training takes time; dogs learn at different paces.
- Ignoring Individual Differences – A method that works for one dog may not work for another.
- Reinforcing Unwanted Behaviors – Accidentally rewarding bad behavior (e.g., giving attention when a dog jumps) can reinforce it.

The right training method can make all the difference in shaping your dog's behavior, confidence, and trust in you. By understanding your dog's needs, using positive reinforcement, and remaining consistent, you can create a training experience that is both effective and enjoyable.

Training is not just about commands; it's about building a strong, lasting relationship with your dog based on communication, respect, and mutual understanding. Choose a method that aligns with your dog's personality and your own training philosophy, and watch as your bond with your furry companion grows stronger each day.

Understanding Your Dog's Breed, Temperament, and Natural Instincts

Every dog is unique, shaped by its genetic heritage, personality, and instincts. Understanding your dog's breed characteristics, temperament, and natural instincts is crucial for effective training and proper care. When you recognize why your dog behaves a certain way, you can tailor training techniques that align with their innate tendencies, making the learning process smoother and more enjoyable for both of you.

The Role of Breed in Training and Behavior

A dog's breed significantly impacts its behavior, energy levels, and learning capabilities. While every dog has an individual personality, breed-specific tendencies can shape how they respond to training and interact with their environment.

Breed Groups and Their General Characteristics

Different dog breeds were originally developed for specific tasks. Understanding the history and purpose of your dog's breed can provide insight into their natural behaviors and training needs.

1. Herding Dogs (Border Collies, Australian Shepherds, German Shepherds, Corgis, etc.)

- Purpose: These dogs were bred to herd livestock by using their intelligence, problem-solving skills, and high energy levels.
- Common Traits: Intelligent, energetic, eager to learn, sometimes overly alert.
- Training Tips: They need mental stimulation, structured training, and tasks that mimic their herding instincts (such as agility training or advanced obedience work).

2. Working Dogs (Rottweilers, Boxers, Dobermans, Siberian Huskies, etc.)

- Purpose: Bred for jobs such as guarding, pulling sleds, or rescue work.
- Common Traits: Strong, confident, protective, and highly trainable.
- Training Tips: Consistent leadership is necessary. They respond well to advanced obedience training, protection training, and structured routines.

3. Sporting Dogs (Labrador Retrievers, Golden Retrievers, Spaniels, Setters, etc.)

- Purpose: Developed to retrieve game in hunting environments, these dogs have strong retrieving instincts and love water.
- Common Traits: Friendly, intelligent, eager to please, high energy.
- Training Tips: They excel with positive reinforcement, need plenty of exercise, and enjoy retrieving games like fetch.

4. Hound Dogs (Beagles, Bloodhounds, Dachshunds, Greyhounds, etc.)

- Purpose: Used for tracking scents, hunting, or chasing prey.
- Common Traits: Stubborn, independent, strong prey drive, highly focused.
- Training Tips: Training requires patience. Use scent-based activities and rewards that appeal to their tracking instincts.

5. Terrier Breeds (Jack Russell Terrier, Bull Terrier, Scottish Terrier, etc.)

- Purpose: Originally bred for hunting vermin.
- Common Traits: Energetic, feisty, independent, high prey drive.
- Training Tips: Short, engaging training sessions work best. They need outlets for their energy, such as interactive play or digging areas.

6. Toy Breeds (Chihuahua, Pomeranian, Maltese, Pekingese, etc.)

- Purpose: Bred primarily for companionship rather than work.
- Common Traits: Loyal, alert, affectionate, sometimes stubborn.
- Training Tips: Socialization is key to prevent excessive barking or nervousness. Reward-based training is highly effective.

7. Non-Sporting Breeds (Bulldogs, Dalmatians, Poodles, Shiba Inu, etc.)

- Purpose: A diverse group with varying characteristics.
- Common Traits: Temperaments range from laid-back to energetic.
- Training Tips: Understand their individual personality and adjust training methods accordingly.

8. Mixed Breeds and Rescue Dogs

- Purpose: May inherit traits from multiple breeds.
- Common Traits: Vary widely in temperament, intelligence, and energy.
- Training Tips: Observe behavior patterns and cater training to their strengths and instincts.

How Temperament Affects Training

Temperament is the combination of a dog's natural personality, emotional tendencies, and behavioral traits. Unlike breed characteristics, temperament is unique to each dog and can be influenced by genetics, early socialization, and environment.

Key Temperament Traits and Their Impact on Training

1. Confident Dogs

- Eager to take charge, may try to dominate if not properly trained.
- Respond well to firm but fair leadership.
- Require structured training to establish boundaries.
2. Shy or Timid Dogs
    - Can be fearful in new situations, sensitive to corrections.
    - Need gentle encouragement and positive reinforcement.
    - Benefit from slow, patient socialization and exposure to new experiences.
3. Energetic and Hyperactive Dogs
    - Require more physical and mental exercise to stay focused.
    - Thrive with engaging training sessions and structured routines.
    - May need impulse control exercises, such as "wait" or "stay" commands.
4. Independent and Stubborn Dogs
    - Often found in breeds with strong hunting or guarding instincts.
    - Need extra motivation (high-value treats, favorite toys).
    - Short, consistent training sessions work best.
5. Eager-to-Please Dogs
    - Quick learners who respond well to positive reinforcement.
    - Easy to train but may become too dependent on rewards.
    - Training should include verbal praise and affection in addition to treats.

Understanding Natural Instincts and Their Impact on Behavior

Dogs retain instincts from their wild ancestors. Recognizing these instincts helps guide training and prevent behavioral issues.

Common Instincts in Dogs

1. Pack Mentality
    - Dogs naturally seek leadership and structure.
    - Establishing yourself as a calm and assertive leader is crucial.
2. Prey Drive
    - Some breeds (such as terriers and hounds) have strong prey instincts.
    - Training recall and impulse control can prevent chasing behaviors.
3. Territorial Behavior
    - Guarding breeds may instinctively protect their home and family.
    - Early socialization reduces overprotectiveness.
4. Chewing and Digging
    - Natural behaviors for relieving stress or seeking entertainment.
    - Providing chew toys and designated digging areas prevents destruction.
5. Herding and Nipping
    - Common in herding breeds, which may try to "herd" children or other pets.

- o   Redirection training helps channel these instincts appropriately.
6. Barking and Vocalization
   - o   Some breeds (like Beagles or Huskies) are naturally more vocal.
   - o   Teaching a "quiet" command helps manage excessive barking.

How to Adapt Training Based on Your Dog's Traits

Once you understand your dog's breed, temperament, and instincts, training should be adjusted accordingly.

- For High-Energy Breeds – Provide extra exercise, use mentally stimulating training like agility.
- For Stubborn Breeds – Keep training sessions short and use high-value rewards.
- For Shy Dogs – Build confidence through gentle, reward-based training and socialization.
- For Guarding Breeds – Start socialization early to prevent excessive protectiveness.
- For Hunting Dogs – Use scent-based games and tracking exercises.

A successful training approach begins with understanding your dog's unique combination of breed tendencies, temperament, and natural instincts. No single training method works for all dogs—adjustments must be made based on your dog's personality and learning style.

Creating a Positive Training Environment

A dog's ability to learn is deeply influenced by its surroundings, emotions, and the relationship it shares with its owner. A well-structured, positive training environment ensures that the dog feels secure, motivated, and eager to engage in learning. Training should never be about fear, dominance, or punishment—it should be built on mutual trust, encouragement, and consistency. Establishing the right environment will help lay a strong foundation for obedience, behavior shaping, and lifelong good habits.

The Role of a Safe and Comfortable Space

Dogs thrive in an environment where they feel safe, relaxed, and focused. Before training begins, it's important to set up a dedicated space that minimizes distractions and maximizes the opportunity for learning.

A training area should be quiet, free from excessive noise, and spacious enough for movement-based commands. If training takes place indoors, choose a location with minimal foot traffic and away from televisions, other pets, or anything that may divert attention. If training occurs outdoors, opt for a fenced or enclosed space to reduce the risk of wandering or external distractions such as cars, people, or other animals.

Lighting and flooring also play a role in the dog's ability to focus. A well-lit area allows for clear visual communication, while non-slippery surfaces prevent injury, especially during movement-based training. Comfortable temperatures should also be maintained so the dog is neither too hot nor too cold, as discomfort can reduce attention span and engagement.

Building a Trusting Relationship Before Training

A dog's willingness to learn is directly linked to its trust in its owner. Without a bond built on trust, training can become frustrating for both the dog and the trainer. The key to developing this relationship is patience, positive reinforcement, and daily interaction that strengthens the bond.

Dogs feel more confident in an environment where they are not afraid of being punished or scolded. Harsh discipline, raised voices, or intimidating behavior can lead to fear, making training ineffective. Instead, reinforcing positive behaviors through encouragement and rewards builds confidence and deepens the connection between dog and owner.

Trust is strengthened through regular interaction, playtime, and consistent daily routines. Engaging in non-training activities such as walks, interactive games, and gentle petting fosters a sense of security. The more a dog trusts its owner, the more willing it will be to learn, follow commands, and enjoy the training process.

Consistency and Routine in Training

Dogs learn best through consistency. Having a structured routine establishes clear expectations, making it easier for them to grasp new commands and behaviors. Training should take place at the same time each day whenever possible, as dogs adapt well to predictable schedules.

A consistent approach also applies to cues, rewards, and corrections. Using the same command words and hand signals for each action prevents confusion. If multiple people are involved in the training process, everyone should use identical verbal cues and gestures to reinforce learning.

Dogs respond better when they understand what is expected of them. Mixed messages, shifting rules, or inconsistent responses to behaviors can cause confusion. If a dog is allowed on the couch one day and then scolded for it the next, it will struggle to understand what is right or wrong. Setting clear and unchanging rules helps the dog feel secure in its training environment.

Using Positive Reinforcement as a Core Training Principle

A positive training environment relies on reinforcement rather than punishment. Rewarding good behavior encourages the dog to repeat those actions, reinforcing learning in a way that is enjoyable and stress-free.

Treats, praise, and affection serve as powerful motivators. Every dog has different preferences, so finding the most effective reward is essential. Some dogs respond best to food-based rewards, while others prefer verbal encouragement or playtime with their favorite toy.

Timing is crucial when rewarding behavior. A reward should be given immediately after the desired action to help the dog associate the behavior with the positive outcome. Delayed rewards may cause confusion and weaken the effectiveness of reinforcement.

Using an enthusiastic and encouraging tone of voice also enhances the reward process. Dogs respond well to positive energy and excitement, making training feel like a fun and engaging activity rather than a strict obligation.

Minimizing Stress and Frustration During Training

Frustration can hinder a dog's ability to learn and may even create anxiety that makes training more difficult. A dog should never feel pressured or overwhelmed. If a dog struggles to understand a command, patience is essential. Repeating the exercise calmly, adjusting techniques, and allowing the dog time to process new information prevents stress.

Short training sessions prevent mental fatigue. Overly long sessions can cause boredom or frustration, making the dog less responsive. Training should be broken into manageable sessions, followed by breaks that allow the dog to relax and absorb what it has learned.

Recognizing signs of stress, such as excessive yawning, licking lips, or avoiding eye contact, helps identify when a dog may need a break. Pushing a stressed or unresponsive dog to continue training can lead to negative associations, reducing enthusiasm for future sessions.

Eliminating Distractions for Better Focus

A focused dog is a successful learner. Distractions can make it difficult for a dog to concentrate, especially in the early stages of training. The level of distraction should be gradually increased as the dog becomes more proficient in following commands.

Beginning training in a controlled, distraction-free setting allows the dog to fully engage with the learning process. As skills improve, training can transition to environments with moderate distractions, such as a backyard or a quiet park. Eventually, training in busier areas will help reinforce obedience in real-world situations.

During training, limiting background noise and removing unnecessary stimuli makes it easier for the dog to listen and respond to commands. If another pet or family member is nearby, ensuring they remain still and quiet helps maintain focus.

Distraction training is also valuable in reinforcing obedience. Once the dog has mastered a command in a calm setting, introducing mild distractions teaches them to remain focused under different conditions. For example, practicing "sit" or "stay" while a toy is placed nearby strengthens impulse control.

Using the Right Training Equipment

The correct training tools help create a positive learning environment. The choice of equipment should be based on comfort, effectiveness, and the specific needs of the dog.

A comfortable collar or harness is essential for leash training. Tight or restrictive equipment can cause discomfort, leading to resistance and negative associations. A well-fitted leash provides control while allowing enough freedom for movement.

Clickers are useful for marking correct behaviors with precision, especially when used consistently with rewards. They provide immediate feedback, helping the dog understand exactly what behavior is being reinforced.

Soft, high-value treats encourage motivation, while interactive toys add an element of playfulness to training. Having a designated reward system tailored to the dog's preferences makes training more engaging and enjoyable.

Encouraging a Lifetime of Learning

A positive training environment extends beyond basic obedience lessons. Training should be an ongoing, lifelong process that continuously reinforces good behavior. Keeping training sessions lighthearted, engaging, and rewarding strengthens the bond between dog and owner while ensuring long-term behavioral success.

Making learning enjoyable prevents training from feeling like a chore. Integrating training into daily activities, such as practicing commands during walks or playtime, maintains consistency. Introducing new challenges or tricks keeps the dog mentally stimulated and eager to learn.

A dog that enjoys training will remain receptive to learning new skills throughout its life. By fostering an environment that prioritizes encouragement, patience, and trust, training becomes a fulfilling and rewarding experience for both the dog and the owner.

Essential Training Tools and Equipment

Training a dog effectively requires the right tools and equipment to enhance communication, reinforce positive behaviors, and ensure safety. While training techniques play a crucial role, having the proper gear can significantly improve the learning experience for both the dog and the trainer. Selecting the right tools depends on the dog's breed, temperament, and training goals. Using the correct equipment helps establish a strong foundation for obedience, behavior correction, and advanced training.

A well-equipped trainer is a prepared trainer. Investing in high-quality tools ensures training sessions are productive, engaging, and enjoyable for both the dog and the owner. This guide explores essential training tools and how to use them effectively.

Collars and Harnesses: Choosing the Right Fit for Training

A collar or harness is one of the first training tools a dog will use. Selecting the right one is essential for comfort, safety, and control during training. Different types of collars and harnesses serve various purposes, and using the appropriate option can make training easier.

Standard Flat Collar

The most commonly used collar, a flat collar, is ideal for everyday use and basic training. It should fit snugly without being too tight, allowing two fingers to slide between the collar and the dog's neck. A well-fitted flat collar is suitable for teaching commands like sit, stay, and recall.

Martingale Collar

Designed to prevent a dog from slipping out of its collar, a martingale collar tightens slightly when the dog pulls but does not choke. This collar is especially useful for dogs with narrow heads, such as Greyhounds and Whippets, and for leash training.

Harnesses

Harnesses are a great alternative to collars, particularly for dogs prone to pulling or those with respiratory issues. They distribute pressure across the chest rather than the neck, reducing strain and increasing comfort.

- Front-Clip Harness: Helps reduce pulling by redirecting the dog's movement toward the owner.
- Back-Clip Harness: Ideal for well-trained dogs, as it offers comfort and freedom of movement.
- Dual-Clip Harness: Provides both front and back attachment points, allowing for greater control and versatility in training.

Head Collars (Gentle Leaders or Halti Collars)

These collars fit around the dog's muzzle and give the handler more control over the head, making them useful for managing strong or reactive dogs. When the dog pulls, the head collar gently guides the nose downward, discouraging pulling without causing pain. Proper introduction and gradual acclimation are necessary to ensure the dog is comfortable wearing it.

Leashes: The Key to Control and Safety

A good leash provides control, safety, and a direct line of communication between the dog and the trainer. Choosing the right type of leash depends on the training goals and the environment in which training takes place.

Standard Leash (4-6 Feet)

A sturdy, fixed-length leash made of nylon or leather is ideal for everyday walks and obedience training. It provides enough freedom for movement while ensuring the handler maintains control.

Long Line (15-30 Feet)

Used for recall training and off-leash preparation, a long line allows the dog to explore while still being under control. It is useful for teaching distance commands and reinforcing obedience in open spaces.

Retractable Leash

A retractable leash extends and retracts, giving dogs more freedom. However, it is not ideal for training, as it encourages pulling and can cause injuries if not used properly. Fixed-length leashes are better suited for structured training sessions.

Slip Lead

A leash and collar combination that tightens when the dog pulls, a slip lead is commonly used for quick training corrections. While effective, it should only be used under supervision to prevent excessive pressure on the neck.

Training Treats and Reward Systems

Positive reinforcement is one of the most effective training methods, and treats are a powerful motivator. Choosing the right type of reward can enhance training success.

High-Value Treats

These treats are highly desirable to dogs and should be used for teaching new commands or reinforcing difficult behaviors. Examples include small pieces of cooked chicken, cheese, or freeze-dried liver.

Low-Value Treats

Less enticing but still rewarding, these treats are suitable for simple tasks the dog has already mastered. Kibble or dog biscuits can be used for basic reinforcement.

Clicker Training

A clicker is a small device that makes a distinct clicking sound, marking the exact moment a dog performs a desired behavior. The sound is followed by a treat, reinforcing the behavior. Clicker training is highly effective for shaping new behaviors and increasing accuracy.

Verbal Praise and Affection

Not all rewards need to be food-based. Some dogs respond well to verbal praise, petting, or playtime. Finding what motivates a dog the most helps keep training engaging.

Interactive and Training Toys

Toys play a crucial role in keeping training fun and stimulating. They also help redirect unwanted behaviors such as chewing and excessive energy.

Treat-Dispensing Toys

Designed to hold treats or kibble, these toys engage a dog's mind and reward problem-solving. Kong toys and puzzle feeders are excellent options for mental stimulation.

Chew Toys

Chewing is a natural behavior, and providing appropriate chew toys prevents destructive chewing on furniture or shoes. Durable rubber or nylon chews help satisfy a dog's urge to chew.

Rope Toys

Used for tug-of-war games, rope toys strengthen the bond between dog and owner while promoting interactive play.

Scent Work and Nose Training Toys

Encouraging scent work through hide-and-seek games and scent-training toys engages a dog's natural instincts and improves focus.

Crates and Gates for Management and Training

Crates and gates provide structure and security, aiding in housebreaking, travel, and behavior management.

Crates

Crate training helps create a safe space for dogs. When used correctly, a crate is not a punishment but a comforting den. It is especially useful for potty training and reducing separation anxiety.

- Plastic Crates: Enclosed on all sides, offering a den-like feel.
- Wire Crates: Provide better airflow and visibility.
- Soft-Sided Crates: Lightweight and portable, ideal for travel.

Baby Gates and Exercise Pens

Used to create boundaries, gates and pens help manage movement within the home. They prevent access to restricted areas and provide a safe space for puppies or dogs in training.

Whistles, Training Aids, and Specialized Equipment

Additional training tools can help with advanced training, behavior correction, and specialized tasks.

Dog Training Whistle

A whistle provides a consistent sound for recall training, making it useful for off-leash training and working dogs.

Target Stick

Used for trick training and shaping behaviors, a target stick helps guide a dog's movement with precision.

Vibration Collars

Used for deaf dogs or as an alternative to verbal commands, vibration collars gently signal the dog to gain attention.

Treat Pouch

A hands-free way to carry treats, a treat pouch allows for quick reward delivery during training sessions.

Having the right training tools and equipment enhances the learning experience, ensuring training sessions are effective, engaging, and stress-free. The key to success lies in selecting tools that align with the dog's individual needs, temperament, and training goals. Whether using a well-fitted harness, interactive toys, or positive reinforcement techniques, each tool plays a role in shaping a well-behaved and confident dog.

Establishing Leadership: Becoming a Confident Pack Leader

A well-trained dog is not just the result of commands and treats; it is the product of a strong, confident, and consistent leader. Dogs are instinctively pack animals, and they look to their owners for guidance, protection, and structure. Without clear leadership, a dog may develop behavioral problems such as excessive barking, leash pulling, dominance, aggression, or anxiety. Establishing yourself as a confident pack leader is not about being forceful or authoritarian; rather, it is about earning your dog's trust and respect through consistency, patience, and positive reinforcement.

The key to a well-balanced dog is leadership. A dog that understands its place in the home is more likely to feel secure, behave well, and respond to training. Here's how to establish leadership in a way that strengthens your bond and promotes a harmonious relationship with your dog.

Understanding the Concept of Leadership in Dog Training

Leadership in the canine world is based on trust, consistency, and clear communication. Dogs thrive when they understand their role within the family structure. In the wild, dogs rely on a hierarchy within their pack for survival. The leader of the pack makes important decisions about food, safety, and movement. In a domestic setting, a dog still looks for structure and guidance from its human family.

When a dog senses uncertainty or inconsistency from its owner, it may assume the leadership role, leading to undesirable behaviors such as excessive guarding, possessiveness, leash pulling, or even aggressive tendencies. A strong leader provides direction without intimidation, ensuring that the dog feels secure and understands what is expected.

The most effective leaders:

- Are calm and assertive – A leader does not react emotionally to a dog's behavior but instead remains steady, confident, and composed.
- Set clear rules and boundaries – Dogs feel safe when they know what is allowed and what is not.
- Are consistent in training and expectations – Changing rules or being inconsistent can confuse a dog and cause behavioral issues.
- Use positive reinforcement – Rewarding good behavior strengthens a dog's trust and respect.

- Provide structure in daily routines – A predictable schedule helps dogs feel more secure and reduces anxiety.

Building Trust Through Calm, Assertive Energy

Dogs are highly perceptive animals and respond to human emotions, body language, and tone of voice. If you are anxious, nervous, or overly excitable, your dog will pick up on these emotions and may become unsettled or reactive. A strong leader exudes calm confidence, creating an environment of stability and trust.

- Avoid yelling or harsh corrections – Dogs do not respond well to fear-based leadership. Instead, use a firm but calm voice when giving commands.
- Control your emotions – If a dog senses frustration or anger, it may become fearful or resistant. Training should always be approached with patience and a positive mindset.
- Stand tall and use confident body language – Dogs read body language more than verbal cues. Standing upright with shoulders back and making eye contact (without staring aggressively) signals authority.
- Move with purpose – Avoid hesitation or uncertain movements, as dogs interpret this as weakness. When walking your dog or giving a command, be deliberate in your actions.

A dog that trusts its owner as a leader will naturally look to them for guidance and reassurance, making training and socialization much easier.

Setting Boundaries and Rules for a Well-Behaved Dog

Just like children, dogs thrive in an environment with clear rules and expectations. Without structure, dogs may become confused and try to establish their own rules. This can lead to behavioral problems such as jumping on guests, begging at the table, or refusing to follow commands.

Establishing boundaries teaches a dog to respect personal space, household rules, and social etiquette.

Ways to Set and Reinforce Rules

- Control access to food – Leaders always eat first in a pack. Teach your dog to wait patiently while you prepare food and only allow them to eat after you give permission.
- Decide when play begins and ends – Initiate and end playtime to reinforce that you are in charge. If a dog becomes overly excited, stop the game until it calms down.
- Manage doorways and entrances – Always walk through doors first and teach your dog to wait for permission before entering or exiting. This establishes control and prevents excessive pulling or rushing ahead.
- No free access to furniture (if desired) – If you prefer your dog not to be on furniture, establish this rule early on. If allowed, ensure the dog understands it is a privilege, not a right.

- Teach a solid "wait" or "stay" command – This reinforces impulse control and respect for your authority.

Being firm and consistent with boundaries prevents confusion and ensures your dog understands what is expected.

Consistency: The Foundation of Strong Leadership

Dogs do not understand exceptions to the rules. If a behavior is sometimes allowed and other times discouraged, it creates confusion and frustration. Consistency in rules, commands, and expectations is crucial for reinforcing leadership.

How to Stay Consistent in Leadership

- Use the same commands – If you teach "down" one day and "lie down" the next, your dog may not understand they mean the same thing. Stick to clear, concise commands.
- Enforce rules every time – If begging at the table is not allowed, it must never be allowed, not even as a special treat.
- Reward good behavior consistently – Praise or reward should immediately follow positive behavior to reinforce it effectively.
- Ensure all family members follow the same rules – A dog will quickly learn to take advantage of inconsistencies. If one person allows jumping and another discourages it, the dog will become confused.

A strong leader provides consistent guidance, helping a dog feel secure and reinforcing good behavior.

Leading on Walks: The Importance of Leash Leadership

Daily walks are an essential opportunity to reinforce leadership. A well-trained dog should walk politely on a loose leash without pulling or dictating the pace. Allowing a dog to drag its owner or take charge of the walk sends the message that it is the leader.

How to Establish Leadership on Walks

- Start walks calmly – If a dog is excited before the walk begins, wait for it to settle before putting on the leash.
- Walk with purpose and confidence – Lead the walk by stepping out first and maintaining a steady pace.
- Keep the leash short but relaxed – A tense leash can signal stress, while a loose leash promotes calm behavior.
- Correct pulling immediately – If a dog pulls, stop walking and wait until it refocuses before continuing. Reward loose leash walking with treats and praise.

By reinforcing leadership during walks, dogs learn to respect their owner's guidance both inside and outside the home.

The Role of Mental Stimulation and Training in Leadership

A mentally engaged dog is less likely to develop problem behaviors. Leadership is not just about controlling a dog's actions; it is also about providing structure and enrichment.

Ways to Mentally Challenge a Dog

- Obedience training – Practicing commands daily reinforces structure and discipline.
- Puzzle toys and scent work – Encouraging problem-solving through games engages a dog's brain.
- Structured play sessions – Interactive games like fetch, hide-and-seek, or agility training provide both exercise and mental stimulation.

By offering guidance and engaging activities, a leader ensures a dog remains happy, well-behaved, and eager to learn.

Being a confident pack leader is not about dominance or control; it is about guiding a dog with patience, structure, and respect. A well-led dog is a happy and secure dog, eager to please and responsive to training.

Chapter 2: Puppy Training Foundations

The early stages of a puppy's life are crucial for shaping behavior, building trust, and ensuring lifelong obedience. With patience, consistency, and positive reinforcement, you can guide your puppy toward becoming a well-mannered, confident, and happy companion.

The Critical Socialization Period: What to Do and What to Avoid

Socialization is one of the most important aspects of raising a well-adjusted and confident dog. The critical socialization period occurs during a puppy's early developmental stage, typically between three and sixteen weeks of age. During this time, puppies are highly impressionable, forming lifelong associations with people, animals, environments, sounds, and experiences. Proper socialization helps prevent behavioral problems such as fear, aggression, and anxiety, ensuring that your dog grows into a friendly and adaptable companion.

Understanding what to do and what to avoid during this critical period is essential for effective socialization. A well-socialized puppy will be comfortable in new situations, confident around people and animals, and less likely to develop fear-based behavioral problems later in life.

Why the Critical Socialization Period Matters

The experiences a puppy has during this phase will shape their personality and behavior for the rest of their life. Puppies who are properly socialized are more likely to develop into well-mannered, relaxed, and friendly dogs. On the other hand, puppies who miss out on socialization or have negative experiences may grow into fearful, anxious, or reactive dogs.

Many behavioral issues, such as aggression toward strangers, fear of loud noises, separation anxiety, and difficulty adapting to change, stem from inadequate socialization. By exposing your puppy to various experiences in a safe and controlled manner, you help them build confidence and resilience.

What to Do During the Critical Socialization Period

Introduce Your Puppy to a Variety of People

Expose your puppy to people of different ages, appearances, and voices, including men, women, children, elderly individuals, and people wearing hats, sunglasses, or carrying umbrellas. This helps them feel comfortable around all types of individuals rather than developing fear or hesitation toward unfamiliar people.

Expose Your Puppy to Different Environments

Take your puppy to various places such as parks, sidewalks, pet-friendly stores, and different types of terrain like grass, pavement, sand, and wooden floors. This exposure helps them adapt to different surroundings and prevents fear of new environments.

Introduce Your Puppy to Other Friendly Dogs and Animals

Socialization with other dogs and animals is essential. Arrange safe and controlled playdates with well-behaved, vaccinated dogs to teach your puppy proper canine communication. Exposing them to other animals, such as cats, birds, and livestock (if applicable), will also help them learn to coexist peacefully.

Expose Your Puppy to Different Sounds

Introduce your puppy to a variety of sounds, including household noises (vacuum cleaner, doorbell, television), outdoor noises (traffic, sirens, fireworks), and different types of music or human voices. Gradual exposure to these sounds helps prevent noise-related anxieties later in life.

Encourage Positive Handling Experiences

Get your puppy comfortable with being touched, groomed, and examined. Regularly handle their paws, ears, and mouth to prepare them for future grooming and veterinary visits. This helps reduce fear of being handled by humans.

Use Positive Reinforcement

Reward your puppy with treats, praise, and affection when they react calmly to new experiences. Positive reinforcement creates a strong association between new stimuli and positive outcomes, encouraging your puppy to feel safe and confident.

Expose Your Puppy to Different Objects and Situations

Introduce your puppy to moving objects such as bicycles, skateboards, and wheelchairs so they become familiar with them. Let them experience situations like car rides, elevators, and crowds to help them develop adaptability.

What to Avoid During the Critical Socialization Period

Forcing Your Puppy Into Overwhelming Situations

Socialization should be a gradual and positive experience. Forcing your puppy into overwhelming situations, such as a crowded event or a loud, chaotic environment, can create fear instead of confidence. Allow them to explore at their own pace while providing reassurance.

Exposing Your Puppy to Unvaccinated or Aggressive Dogs

While socializing with other dogs is crucial, interactions must be safe. Avoid exposing your puppy to unvaccinated or aggressive dogs, as this can lead to negative experiences or even illness. Choose well-behaved and vaccinated playmates for positive interactions.

Neglecting to Supervise Interactions

Always supervise your puppy's interactions with other animals and people. Unsupervised play can lead to rough handling, negative experiences, or fear development if a situation becomes overwhelming for your puppy.

Ignoring Signs of Fear or Stress

If your puppy appears fearful—showing signs such as cowering, tail tucking, lip licking, or trying to escape—do not force them to stay in the situation. Instead, remove them and try again later with a gentler approach. Ignoring fear can cause long-term anxiety.

Socializing Too Late

The longer you wait to socialize your puppy, the more difficult it will be to correct behavioral issues that arise from lack of exposure. Missing the critical socialization period may result in lifelong fears, anxieties, or aggression toward unfamiliar people, animals, or situations.

Exposing Your Puppy to Negative Experiences

Avoid situations where your puppy might feel threatened or scared, such as harsh handling, exposure to aggressive animals, or punishment-based training. Negative experiences during this period can leave lasting emotional scars, making training and socialization more challenging in the future.

Creating a Positive Socialization Plan

To ensure your puppy is socialized properly, create a structured plan with gradual exposure to different stimuli. Keep socialization sessions short and positive, gradually increasing their complexity over time. Here's a general guide:

- Introduce one new experience at a time
- Keep interactions brief and pleasant
- Reward calm and confident behavior with treats and praise
- Avoid overwhelming or stressful situations
- Observe body language for signs of fear or discomfort

A well-planned socialization routine will set the stage for a lifetime of positive interactions and adaptability.

The critical socialization period is a short yet crucial window in your puppy's development that determines how they will interact with the world for the rest of their life.

Avoid negative experiences, do not rush the process, and always use positive reinforcement. A well-socialized puppy will be more adaptable, less fearful, and better equipped to handle life's challenges, making them a joy to have as a lifelong companion.

Basic Puppy Obedience: Teaching Name Recognition, Sit, Stay, and Come

Training a puppy in basic obedience is one of the most rewarding aspects of pet ownership. Establishing fundamental commands such as name recognition, sit, stay, and come not only makes daily interactions easier but also lays the groundwork for advanced training and good behavior throughout your dog's life. These basic commands help prevent behavioral issues, keep your puppy safe, and strengthen the bond between you and your furry companion.

Puppies are eager to learn, and with the right approach—one that incorporates patience, consistency, and positive reinforcement—they can master these essential obedience commands relatively quickly.

Teaching Name Recognition

Before introducing any formal commands, it's crucial that your puppy learns to recognize and respond to their name. Name recognition is the foundation of all training because it helps capture your puppy's attention and ensures they focus on you when called.

Step-by-Step Training Process

1. Choose a Clear, Distinct Name
    - Pick a name that is short, simple, and easy to pronounce. Avoid names that sound similar to common commands (e.g., "Kit" sounds like "Sit").
2. Create a Positive Association
    - Say your puppy's name in a happy and inviting tone.
    - The moment they look at you, reward them with a treat and praise.

3. Use Name Recognition in Daily Activities
   - Call their name before giving them food, playtime, or affection.
   - Encourage family members to reinforce name recognition by using the puppy's name in a positive context.
4. Practice in Different Environments
   - Start training in a quiet area with minimal distractions.
   - Gradually increase difficulty by practicing in various settings, such as the backyard, the park, or near other people and pets.
5. Avoid Overuse or Negative Associations
   - Never use your puppy's name in a scolding or angry tone.
   - Avoid overusing their name without giving a reward, as they might start ignoring it.

With consistent reinforcement, your puppy will learn that responding to their name leads to positive outcomes, setting the stage for other obedience training.

Teaching the "Sit" Command

"Sit" is one of the easiest and most useful commands to teach a puppy. It's a natural behavior that can be reinforced quickly, and it helps manage hyperactivity, jumping, and excitement.

Step-by-Step Training Process

1. Get Your Puppy's Attention
   - Hold a treat in front of your puppy's nose to engage their focus.
2. Lure the Puppy into a Sitting Position
   - Slowly move the treat upward over their head.
   - As their head follows the treat, their bottom will naturally lower to the ground.
3. Say "Sit" and Reward
   - As soon as your puppy sits, say "Sit" in a firm but cheerful tone.
   - Immediately give them the treat and praise.
4. Repeat and Reinforce
   - Practice multiple times a day in short, fun sessions.
   - Gradually increase the duration of the sit before giving the treat.
5. Introduce Hand Signals and Fade Treats
   - Pair a hand signal (like raising your palm) with the verbal command.
   - Eventually, reduce treat frequency but continue using praise and affection.
6. Practice in Different Situations
   - Reinforce the command in various settings to ensure your puppy obeys in any environment.

Teaching "sit" helps calm excited puppies and provides a foundation for other commands, such as "stay" and "wait."

Teaching the "Stay" Command

The "stay" command teaches impulse control and prevents your puppy from bolting, running into danger, or behaving disruptively.

Step-by-Step Training Process

1. Start with the "Sit" Command
    - Ask your puppy to sit before introducing "stay."
2. Give the "Stay" Command
    - With your puppy sitting, say "Stay" while holding your palm out in a stop gesture.
3. Take a Small Step Back
    - If your puppy remains in place, quickly reward them with a treat and praise.
    - If they move, calmly reset them into a sit and try again.
4. Gradually Increase Distance and Duration
    - Start with just a few seconds before rewarding.
    - Slowly increase the duration and step farther away each time.
5. Use Release Words
    - Introduce a release word like "Okay" or "Free" so your puppy knows when they are allowed to move.
6. Practice in Different Environments
    - Work on "stay" in places with mild distractions before progressing to more challenging settings.

Building a reliable "stay" takes patience, but once mastered, it becomes a powerful tool for managing your puppy's behavior in real-world scenarios.

Teaching the "Come" Command

A strong recall (the ability to return when called) is one of the most crucial commands for a puppy's safety. Teaching "come" ensures your puppy will return to you in any situation, preventing accidents and dangerous situations.

Step-by-Step Training Process

1. Use a Happy and Exciting Tone
    - Say your puppy's name followed by "Come!" in an enthusiastic voice.
    - Squat down, open your arms, and encourage them with positive body language.
2. Reward Immediately
    - When your puppy comes to you, offer a treat, praise, and affection.
    - Ensure that coming to you is always a positive experience.

3. Start in a Low-Distraction Environment
    - Begin in a quiet indoor space before progressing to areas with more distractions.
4. Use a Long Leash for Outdoor Training
    - A long training leash allows you to practice recall in safe, controlled settings.
    - If your puppy hesitates, gently guide them toward you while saying "Come."
5. Never Use "Come" for Punishment
    - Never call your puppy to "Come" if you plan to scold them or end a fun activity.
    - Always associate the command with positive rewards.
6. Increase Distance and Difficulty Gradually
    - Once your puppy reliably comes in easy situations, challenge them by calling from another room or outdoors.

With consistent practice, "come" becomes a life-saving command that ensures your puppy always returns to you, even in distracting or emergency situations.

Teaching basic obedience commands like name recognition, sit, stay, and come lays the groundwork for a well-behaved and responsive dog. These essential skills create a strong bond between you and your puppy, enhance their safety, and prevent common behavioral issues.

The key to successful training is patience, positive reinforcement, and consistency. Keep sessions short and enjoyable, use treats and praise generously, and gradually introduce distractions as your puppy progresses.

Crate Training and Housebreaking: Effective Potty Training Methods

Housebreaking a dog is one of the first and most crucial aspects of training that every dog owner must master. Proper potty training ensures a clean home environment, fosters a positive relationship between the dog and its owner, and helps build good habits that last a lifetime. Among the most effective techniques for housebreaking are crate trainingand potty training methods that establish consistency, patience, and positive reinforcement.

Crate Training

Crate training is a highly effective method that utilizes a dog's natural instincts to create a safe and comfortable space for them. Dogs are naturally den animals, and when introduced properly, a crate becomes their secure retreat rather than a form of punishment.

Benefits of Crate Training

- Aids in Potty Training – Dogs do not like to soil their sleeping area, making crates a useful tool in teaching bladder control and establishing a potty routine.

- Prevents Destructive Behavior – A crate keeps your dog from chewing furniture, shoes, or other household items when unsupervised.
- Encourages Independence – Dogs become comfortable being alone for periods, reducing separation anxiety.
- Facilitates Travel – A crate-trained dog is easier to transport, whether in a car, plane, or new environment.

Choosing the Right Crate

Selecting the appropriate crate size is essential for successful training. The crate should be large enough for your dog to stand, turn around, and lie down comfortably but not too big that they can designate one corner for sleeping and another for eliminating waste.

Crates come in different materials, including:

- Wire Crates – Provide ventilation and visibility; collapsible for easy storage.
- Plastic Crates – Offer more privacy and are great for travel.
- Soft-Sided Crates – Lightweight and portable, ideal for small breeds.
- Heavy-Duty Crates – Best for strong dogs that might attempt to escape.

Introducing Your Dog to the Crate

Crate training should be a positive experience to encourage acceptance. Follow these steps to introduce your dog to their crate:

1. Make the Crate Comfortable – Place soft bedding, blankets, and a few toys inside to create an inviting space.
2. Keep the Door Open Initially – Allow your dog to explore the crate freely without forcing them inside.
3. Use Treats and Positive Reinforcement – Toss treats into the crate to encourage entry and reward calm behavior.
4. Feed Meals in the Crate – Placing food inside helps create a positive association.
5. Gradually Increase Crate Time – Start with short periods and slowly extend the duration as your dog becomes comfortable.

Crate Training Schedule

Consistency is key when using a crate for potty training. Follow a structured schedule based on your dog's age and needs:

- Puppies Under 8 Weeks – Limited crate time, potty breaks every 1–2 hours.
- 8–10 Weeks – Crate for 30 minutes to 1 hour at a time, with frequent potty breaks.

- 10–16 Weeks – Gradually extend crate time; potty breaks every 2–3 hours.
- 4–6 Months – Bladder control improves; crate time increases to 3–4 hours.
- 6+ Months – Most dogs can hold their bladder for 6–8 hours.

Housebreaking Your Dog: Effective Potty Training Methods

Housebreaking, or potty training, teaches dogs where and when it is appropriate to eliminate. A well-planned potty training routine ensures success and minimizes accidents.

Establishing a Potty Routine

Dogs thrive on routine, so creating a structured schedule is essential:

1. Take Your Dog Out Frequently – Puppies need to eliminate after waking up, eating, drinking, playing, or napping.
2. Use the Same Potty Spot – Always take your dog to the same location to reinforce proper behavior.
3. Use a Command Word – Phrases like "Go Potty" or "Do Your Business" help them associate the command with the action.
4. Reward Immediately – Praise and offer treats immediately after they eliminate in the correct place.

Signs Your Dog Needs to Go

Recognizing when your dog needs to eliminate prevents accidents indoors. Common signs include:

- Sniffing the ground
- Circling or whining
- Pacing near the door
- Suddenly stopping play
- Scratching or barking at the door

Indoor Potty Training for Apartments

For those who live in apartments or areas with limited outdoor access, indoor potty training can be an alternative. Options include:

- Pee Pads – Useful for puppies, small breeds, or dogs left alone for long periods.
- Artificial Grass Pads – Mimic outdoor surfaces and are easy to clean.
- Litter Boxes – Some small breeds can be trained to use a litter box.

Preventing Accidents and Correcting Mistakes

Accidents are inevitable during housebreaking, but how you handle them determines your dog's progress.

- Never Punish After the Fact – Dogs do not associate punishment with past actions. Instead, redirect behavior and reinforce proper habits.
- Clean Accidents Thoroughly – Use enzymatic cleaners to remove odors and prevent repeat accidents.
- Interrupt Accidents Immediately – If caught in the act, calmly say "No" and take them outside to finish. Reward success.

Combining Crate Training and Housebreaking for Maximum Success

Using crate training in combination with housebreaking methods creates a well-rounded potty training strategy.

1. Crate Your Dog When Unsupervised – This prevents accidents and reinforces bladder control.
2. Take Your Dog Outside Immediately After Crate Time – Encourage elimination right after release.
3. Maintain a Feeding Schedule – Consistent meal times result in predictable potty habits.
4. Be Patient and Consistent – Every dog learns at their own pace, so avoid frustration.

Troubleshooting Common Potty Training Problems

Puppy Won't Stop Having Accidents

- Ensure they are taken out frequently enough.
- Reduce distractions during potty time.
- Avoid free-roaming in the house before they are trained.

Dog Soils the Crate

- The crate may be too large. Use a divider to limit space.
- Increase potty breaks to avoid prolonged crate time.
- Check for medical issues like urinary tract infections.

Dog Refuses to Go Outside in Bad Weather

- Use a covered area or potty pads indoors during storms.
- Reward extra heavily for braving the weather.
- Invest in a dog raincoat or boots if needed.

Crate training and housebreaking are essential for raising a well-behaved, house-trained dog. Whether using a crate, outdoor training, or indoor methods, the key is consistency and understanding your dog's needs.

Preventing and Correcting Biting, Chewing, and Destructive Behavior

Dogs naturally explore the world using their mouths, but when biting, chewing, and destructive behavior become excessive, they can lead to serious issues. These behaviors often stem from instinct, boredom, anxiety, or a lack of proper training. Understanding the causes and implementing effective training methods can help prevent and correct these behaviors, leading to a well-behaved and happy dog.

Understanding Why Dogs Bite, Chew, and Destroy Objects

Dogs do not engage in destructive behaviors out of spite. Instead, several underlying reasons may contribute to their actions:

- Teething Discomfort – Puppies experience gum pain when teething, leading them to chew on objects for relief.
- Exploratory Behavior – Puppies and young dogs use their mouths to learn about their environment.
- Lack of Training and Socialization – Dogs that haven't been taught proper behaviors may not understand what is acceptable.
- Excess Energy and Boredom – When dogs lack physical and mental stimulation, they may chew or bite to relieve frustration.
- Anxiety and Stress – Dogs with separation anxiety or fear-related stress may chew destructively as a coping mechanism.
- Attention-Seeking – Some dogs learn that chewing or biting gets them attention, even if it's negative.
- Hunger and Nutritional Deficiencies – A lack of proper nutrition may cause dogs to chew on objects in an attempt to find food.

Preventing Biting, Chewing, and Destructive Behavior

The best way to manage unwanted behavior is through prevention. Setting clear rules and providing proper outlets for natural instincts can help maintain a well-behaved dog.

Establishing Boundaries and Rules

- Set clear expectations from the start regarding what is and isn't acceptable behavior.
- Be consistent in enforcing rules to prevent confusion.
- Use commands like "Leave It" and "Drop It" to discourage unwanted chewing and biting.

Providing Proper Chew Toys

- Offer a variety of safe, durable chew toys to satisfy your dog's natural urge to chew.
- Rotate toys regularly to keep them interesting and engaging.

- Choose chew toys that match your dog's size and chewing habits.

Ensuring Sufficient Physical and Mental Stimulation

- Engage in daily exercise, including walks, play sessions, and activities suited to your dog's breed and energy level.
- Provide mental stimulation with interactive toys, puzzle feeders, and training exercises.
- Consider activities like agility training, scent games, or hide-and-seek to keep your dog engaged.

Training Bite Inhibition

Teaching bite inhibition is crucial, especially for puppies. Dogs naturally learn this from their littermates, but reinforcement is necessary:

- If your puppy bites too hard, make a high-pitched "Ouch!" sound and withdraw attention.
- Stop play immediately if biting continues, reinforcing that rough play results in no fun.
- Redirect biting onto appropriate chew toys and reward good behavior.

Using Bitter Sprays and Deterrents

- Apply bitter-tasting sprays to furniture, shoes, or household objects to discourage chewing.
- Always pair deterrents with positive reinforcement so your dog learns what they should chew instead.

Avoiding Reinforcement of Bad Behavior

- Never encourage biting by allowing rough play with hands or feet.
- Avoid dramatic reactions to chewing, as this may make the behavior more rewarding for your dog.
- Do not chase your dog when they steal an object—this turns it into a game. Instead, trade the item for a treat or a toy.

Correcting Biting and Destructive Behavior

If your dog has already developed a habit of biting or chewing inappropriately, corrective training is necessary to redirect their behavior.

Interrupting and Redirecting the Behavior

- When your dog chews on something inappropriate, calmly say "No" or "Leave It."
- Immediately provide an appropriate chew toy and praise them for switching.
- Supervise puppies and young dogs closely to prevent bad habits from forming.

- Use baby gates, crates, or playpens to limit access to areas where destructive chewing occurs.
- Keep household items, shoes, and valuable objects out of reach.

Addressing Anxiety and Stress-Related Chewing

If your dog chews excessively due to anxiety:

- Gradually desensitize them to being alone by starting with short departures and increasing the time gradually.
- Provide comforting items, such as a blanket or t-shirt with your scent.
- Use interactive toys or treat-dispensing puzzles to keep them occupied when alone.

Teaching Alternative Behaviors

For dogs that bite or chew inappropriately, offering alternative behaviors is crucial:

- Train commands such as "Sit" and "Leave It" to encourage self-control.
- Redirect biting onto chew toys and reward proper choices.
- Reinforce calm and appropriate behavior with praise and treats.

Using Positive Reinforcement

- Reward good behavior immediately to strengthen positive associations.
- Avoid punishment-based training, as this can increase fear-based aggression or anxiety.

When to Seek Professional Help

If your dog's biting or destructive chewing persists despite consistent training efforts, professional guidance may be necessary:

- Professional Trainer – If your dog struggles with basic training and behavioral corrections.
- Veterinarian – If sudden chewing or biting develops, ruling out medical conditions is essential.
- Canine Behaviorist – If your dog's behavior is aggressive rather than playful, or if anxiety is severe.

Preventing and correcting biting, chewing, and destructive behavior requires patience, consistency, and a proper understanding of your dog's needs. Providing mental and physical stimulation, clear boundaries, and appropriate training will help curb unwanted habits while fostering a well-behaved and happy companion. With the right approach, your dog can learn to engage in healthy chewing habits and interact safely with people and their environment.

Leash Training for Young Puppies

Leash training is a fundamental skill every puppy needs to learn for safe and enjoyable walks. Teaching your puppy to walk calmly on a leash ensures they can explore their surroundings while remaining under control. Puppies naturally resist leash pressure at first, but with patience, consistency, and positive reinforcement, they can quickly adapt.

Why Leash Training is Important

Leash training provides numerous benefits, both for your puppy and for you:

- Safety and Control – Prevents your puppy from running into traffic, approaching unknown dogs, or getting lost.
- Good Behavior in Public – Teaches your puppy to walk calmly and ignore distractions.
- Socialization Opportunities – Allows your puppy to explore the world while staying under control.
- Prevention of Pulling and Tugging – Early training prevents bad habits from developing.
- Builds a Strong Bond – Strengthens trust and communication between you and your puppy.

Preparing for Leash Training

Choosing the Right Equipment

Selecting the proper leash and collar is essential to make training comfortable and effective:

- Collar or Harness – A soft, adjustable collar or a well-fitted harness is best for young puppies. A harness distributes pressure evenly and prevents strain on the neck.
- Lightweight Leash – A light, four-to-six-foot leash works best for training. Avoid retractable leashes, as they encourage pulling.
- Training Treats – Small, soft treats keep your puppy motivated during training.
- Clicker (Optional) – If you use clicker training, it can help reinforce positive behavior.

Introducing the Collar and Leash

Before starting leash training, help your puppy get used to wearing a collar or harness:

- Let your puppy wear the collar indoors for short periods, gradually increasing the duration.
- Attach the leash and allow them to drag it around under supervision to get accustomed to its weight.
- Give treats and praise when they remain calm while wearing the collar and leash.

Step-by-Step Guide to Leash Training

Step 1: Start Indoors or in a Quiet Area

Before venturing outside, practice leash training in a distraction-free environment:

- Hold the leash loosely and allow your puppy to walk around naturally.
- Call them to you using a happy voice and reward them for following.
- If your puppy resists, avoid pulling—use treats and encouragement instead.

Step 2: Teach 'Come' and 'Follow'

- Encourage your puppy to walk beside you by using a treat in your hand.
- Reward them when they walk in the right direction.
- If they hesitate, take a step back, kneel, and call them gently.

Step 3: Introduce Walking on a Loose Leash

- Start walking a few steps at a time. Reward your puppy for staying close.
- If they pull, stop walking immediately and wait for them to loosen the tension.
- Reward good behavior consistently to reinforce loose-leash walking.

Step 4: Increase Distance and Add Distractions

- Gradually extend your walks, introducing more distractions like new scents, sounds, and other people.
- Practice in different environments, such as parks, sidewalks, or pet-friendly stores.
- Maintain consistency by rewarding good behavior and ignoring pulling.

Common Challenges and How to Solve Them

Pulling on the Leash

- If your puppy pulls, stop walking immediately and wait for them to return to you.
- Reward them when they relax and walk nicely.
- Never yank the leash—use positive reinforcement to teach proper walking habits.

Fear of the Leash

- If your puppy refuses to walk, encourage movement with treats and praise.
- Let them explore their surroundings at their own pace.
- Keep training sessions short and positive to build confidence.

Excessive Stopping and Sniffing

- Allow your puppy to explore but set limits on how long they can stop.
- Use a cue like "Let's go!" to encourage forward movement.
- Reward walking instead of prolonged sniffing.

Lunging at People or Other Dogs

- Distract your puppy with treats before they get overly excited.
- Teach the "Sit" or "Watch Me" command to redirect their focus.
- Increase distance from distractions and gradually decrease it as they improve.

Chewing or Playing with the Leash

- Use a chew-proof leash if necessary.
- Redirect biting behavior with a toy or treat.
- Avoid playing tug-of-war with the leash, as it reinforces bad habits.

Reinforcing Good Leash Behavior

- Practice Daily – Short, consistent training sessions help your puppy develop good habits.
- Use Positive Reinforcement – Reward desired behaviors with praise and treats.
- Stay Patient and Calm – Puppies learn at different rates, so remain patient and avoid frustration.
- Be Consistent – Use the same commands and techniques to prevent confusion.
- End on a Positive Note – Finish each session with praise and rewards to create a positive association with leash walking.

Leash training is an essential skill that requires patience, consistency, and positive reinforcement. By starting early and using gentle techniques, your puppy will learn to walk confidently on a leash, making walks enjoyable for both of you. With regular practice and encouragement, your puppy will develop into a well-behaved and leash-friendly companion.

Chapter 3: Basic Obedience Training

Training your dog in basic obedience builds a strong foundation for good behavior and communication. Teaching essential commands like sit, stay, and recall enhances your bond, ensures safety, and fosters a well-mannered, confident, and happy companion in any environment.

Teaching Essential Commands: Sit, Stay, Down, Come, and Leave It

Training your dog to understand and obey essential commands is crucial for their safety, good behavior, and your overall bond. Commands like Sit, Stay, Down, Come, and Leave It provide structure and help your dog navigate different situations calmly and responsibly. Whether you're raising a puppy or training an older dog, consistency, patience, and positive reinforcement are key to successful learning.

Why Teaching Essential Commands is Important

Mastering basic commands offers multiple benefits for both dogs and their owners:

- Enhances Safety – Commands like Stay and Come can prevent your dog from running into dangerous situations.
- Improves Communication – Clear commands strengthen the bond between you and your dog.
- Prevents Behavioral Problems – Teaching impulse control helps reduce jumping, lunging, and excessive barking.
- Encourages Socialization – Well-trained dogs are more confident and well-behaved in public spaces.
- Makes Everyday Life Easier – Commands help with leash walking, greeting guests, and managing household behavior.

Training Principles for Teaching Commands

Before diving into specific commands, keep these key training principles in mind:

- Use Positive Reinforcement – Reward good behavior with treats, praise, and affection.
- Keep Training Sessions Short – Dogs learn best in short, focused training periods (5–10 minutes).
- Be Consistent – Use the same words and gestures for each command to avoid confusion.
- Train in Different Environments – Gradually introduce distractions to reinforce obedience in various settings.
- End on a Positive Note – Always finish training with success to keep your dog motivated.

Teaching the "Sit" Command

The Sit command is one of the first and easiest commands to teach. It helps control excitement, prevents jumping, and serves as a foundation for other commands.

Step-by-Step Training Guide

1. Get Your Dog's Attention – Hold a treat in front of your dog's nose.
2. Lure into Position – Slowly move the treat upward and slightly backward. As your dog follows, their bottom will naturally lower into a sitting position.
3. Say "Sit" – The moment your dog's bottom touches the ground, say "Sit" in a calm and firm tone.
4. Reward Immediately – Give your dog the treat and praise enthusiastically.
5. Repeat and Practice – Repeat the process multiple times until your dog consistently responds.

Troubleshooting Tips

- If your dog jumps instead of sitting, slow down your hand movement.
- If they struggle, gently guide their hindquarters down while giving the command.
- Practice before meals when your dog is motivated by food.

Teaching the "Stay" Command

The Stay command teaches patience and impulse control, preventing your dog from bolting out the door or running after distractions.

Step-by-Step Training Guide

1. Start in a Sitting Position – Have your dog sit calmly.
2. Give the Stay Command – Hold your palm out like a stop sign and say "Stay."
3. Take a Small Step Back – If your dog remains in place, immediately reward them with a treat and praise.
4. Gradually Increase Distance – Slowly take more steps back while reinforcing the command.
5. Increase Duration – Extend the time your dog stays before giving the reward.
6. Introduce Distractions – Once your dog understands, add small distractions like noises or movement.

Troubleshooting Tips

- If your dog breaks the stay, calmly return them to the original position and try again.
- Use a leash in outdoor settings to maintain control.
- Always release your dog with a cue like "Okay" or "Free" so they know when they can move.

Teaching the "Down" Command

The Down command helps keep your dog calm and relaxed, making it useful for managing excitement or restlessness.

Step-by-Step Training Guide

1. Start with Your Dog Sitting – Have them in a seated position for an easier transition.
2. Use a Treat to Lure Them Down – Hold a treat close to their nose, then slowly lower it to the ground between their paws.
3. Encourage Them to Lie Down – As they follow the treat, their body will naturally lower into a lying position.
4. Say "Down" – Once they are fully lying down, say "Down" clearly.
5. Reward and Praise – Give the treat immediately and praise them warmly.
6. Practice Repeatedly – Gradually increase the duration your dog stays in the down position before rewarding.

Troubleshooting Tips

- If your dog won't lie down, try using a larger treat or a toy to entice them.
- Avoid forcing them down; instead, use patience and encouragement.
- Practice in calm environments before introducing distractions.

Teaching the "Come" Command

The Come command is crucial for recall, ensuring your dog returns to you promptly in any situation.

Step-by-Step Training Guide

1. Start in a Low-Distraction Area – Use an indoor space or a quiet outdoor area with a leash.
2. Crouch and Use an Excited Tone – Say "Come" while opening your arms to encourage your dog.
3. Use Treats or a Favorite Toy – Reward your dog the moment they reach you.
4. Practice on a Long Leash Outdoors – Gradually increase the distance and practice in different settings.
5. Make it Fun – Running backward or using enthusiastic praise makes coming to you rewarding.

Troubleshooting Tips

- Never punish your dog after they come to you, even if they were slow—this creates negative associations.
- If they hesitate, increase motivation with higher-value treats or excited praise.
- Reinforce the command daily, even when not in training mode.

Teaching the "Leave It" Command

The Leave It command prevents dogs from grabbing dangerous or unwanted objects, making it essential for safety.

Step-by-Step Training Guide

1. Hold a Treat in Your Hand – Show your dog the treat but keep it covered in your palm.
2. Say "Leave It" – Wait for them to stop sniffing or pawing at your hand.
3. Reward When They Back Away – The moment they stop trying, give them a different treat from your other hand.
4. Practice with Different Objects – Gradually introduce tempting items like food on the floor or a toy.
5. Increase Difficulty Over Time – Practice in different environments with increasing distractions.

Troubleshooting Tips

- If your dog doesn't respond, use a higher-value reward.
- Always reward with a different item than the one they were told to leave.
- Be patient—some dogs take longer to learn impulse control.

Teaching essential commands like Sit, Stay, Down, Come, and Leave It helps shape a well-behaved and obedient dog. Consistency, patience, and positive reinforcement ensure that training is an enjoyable experience for both you and your dog.

Positive Reinforcement vs. Corrections: Finding the Right Balance

When it comes to training dogs and other pets, the debate between positive reinforcement and corrections is ongoing. Many trainers, behaviorists, and pet owners struggle to find the right balance between rewarding good behavior and correcting undesirable actions. Striking this balance is crucial for effective training, a strong bond between pet and owner, and overall animal well-being.

Understanding both approaches—positive reinforcement and corrections—is essential in order to create a training plan that works for different breeds, personalities, and situations. Each method has its strengths and weaknesses, and their effectiveness often depends on how they are applied.

Understanding Positive Reinforcement

Positive reinforcement is a training method based on rewarding desired behaviors to encourage their repetition. This technique relies on the principle of operant conditioning, where behaviors followed by pleasant consequences are more likely to occur again. Rewards can come in the form of treats, praise, petting, playtime, or anything the dog finds enjoyable.

For example, when a dog sits on command and receives a treat, it learns that sitting results in a positive outcome. Over time, the dog will associate sitting with good things, making it more likely to obey in the future. This method is effective because it builds a positive association with commands and desired behaviors rather than using fear or discomfort.

Benefits of Positive Reinforcement

- Strengthens the Human-Animal Bond: Positive reinforcement fosters trust and enhances the relationship between the pet and its owner. The dog learns that training is a fun and rewarding experience rather than something to fear.
- Encourages a Willing Attitude: Dogs trained with positive reinforcement are often eager to learn because they associate training with pleasant experiences. They become more engaged and motivated to participate.
- Reduces Fear and Anxiety: Using positive reinforcement helps prevent fear-based responses. Dogs that experience fear-free training are more confident and less likely to develop behavioral issues such as aggression or anxiety.
- Effective for All Breeds and Ages: Whether training a young puppy or an older rescue dog, positive reinforcement works across all breeds and life stages. It is adaptable to various learning speeds and personalities.
- Promotes Long-Term Behavior Retention: Dogs trained through positive reinforcement tend to retain learned behaviors more effectively because they associate them with pleasurable outcomes.

Implementing Positive Reinforcement Effectively

To maximize the benefits of positive reinforcement, trainers should consider the following principles:

- Timing is Key: The reward should be given immediately after the desired behavior so the dog makes a clear connection between the action and the reward. Delayed rewards can confuse the animal.
- Consistency Matters: Owners should consistently reward good behavior to reinforce the lesson. If a dog is rewarded for sitting today but ignored for the same behavior tomorrow, it may become confused.
- Use High-Value Rewards: Every dog has different motivators. Some may respond best to treats, while others prefer toys or verbal praise. Understanding what excites the dog can make training more effective.
- Gradual Fading of Treats: While treats are excellent motivators, they should eventually be phased out in favor of praise and other rewards. This ensures that the dog obeys commands even when food is not present.
- Avoid Overfeeding: If treats are frequently used, they should be factored into the dog's daily calorie intake to prevent weight gain. Using small, healthy treats or breaking them into tiny pieces can help.

Understanding Corrections in Training

Corrections, also known as negative reinforcement or punishment, are used to discourage unwanted behaviors. This method can take various forms, such as verbal reprimands, leash corrections, or time-outs. Corrections do not necessarily mean harsh punishment but rather a means of communicating to the dog that a particular behavior is not acceptable.

For example, if a dog jumps on guests and is ignored or turned away (removing attention), it learns that jumping leads to a loss of interaction. Similarly, a quick leash correction when a dog pulls during a walk can serve as a reminder to stay close to its handler.

Types of Corrections

1. Verbal Corrections: Saying "No" or "Ah-ah" in a firm tone to interrupt undesired behavior.
2. Leash Corrections: A quick, gentle tug on the leash to redirect attention or stop pulling.
3. Ignoring Undesirable Behavior: Withholding attention from a dog that is whining or jumping can discourage these actions.
4. Time-Outs: Removing the dog from a rewarding situation if it misbehaves, helping it associate the action with a loss of privilege.
5. Physical Corrections (Minimal and Ethical): Some trainers use gentle physical redirections, such as blocking a dog with their body to prevent lunging. However, excessive force should never be used.

The Risks of Overusing Corrections

While corrections can be effective, excessive or harsh punishment can have negative consequences:

- Creates Fear and Anxiety: If a dog is punished too frequently or too harshly, it may develop fear-based responses, leading to anxiety, avoidance behaviors, or even aggression.
- Damages Trust: A dog that is constantly corrected without positive reinforcement may become wary of its owner, leading to a strained relationship.
- Inconsistent Learning: If corrections are not applied properly, the dog may not understand why it is being punished, leading to confusion and ineffective training.
- Suppresses Behavior Instead of Teaching Alternatives: Corrections alone do not teach dogs what to do instead. For example, punishing a dog for barking may stop the behavior temporarily, but if the root cause (e.g., boredom, anxiety) is not addressed, the barking will continue in different ways.

Finding the Right Balance

A well-balanced training approach incorporates both positive reinforcement and fair corrections. The key is to reward desired behaviors while discouraging unwanted ones in a humane and effective way.

Guidelines for a Balanced Training Approach

- Use Positive Reinforcement as the Primary Method: Start by focusing on rewarding good behavior. Encouraging the dog to make good choices naturally reduces the need for corrections.
- Apply Corrections Fairly and Sparingly: Corrections should be used only when necessary and should be mild enough to serve as a guidance tool rather than a punishment.
- Match Training Methods to the Dog's Personality: Some dogs are highly sensitive and respond poorly to corrections, while others may require firmer guidance. Tailoring training methods to the individual dog ensures better results.
- Always Offer an Alternative Behavior: If correcting an unwanted behavior, provide an alternative action the dog can perform instead. For example, if a dog jumps, redirect it to sit instead.
- Remain Consistent and Clear: Dogs thrive on consistency. All family members should follow the same rules and training techniques to avoid confusion.
- Use Training Tools Responsibly: Leashes, harnesses, clickers, and treats should be used to reinforce positive behaviors rather than as means of excessive control.

The debate between positive reinforcement and corrections is not about choosing one over the other but about finding the right balance. Positive reinforcement should always be the foundation of training, as it promotes a strong bond, encourages willingness to learn, and ensures long-term behavioral retention. However, gentle and fair corrections can be useful in guiding dogs away from undesirable behaviors when used correctly.

The ultimate goal of training is to create a well-mannered, happy, and confident pet that understands expectations and enjoys a positive relationship with its owner.

Using Treats, Toys, and Praise Effectively

Training a dog requires effective communication, motivation, and reinforcement. Among the most powerful tools at a trainer's disposal are treats, toys, and praise. These three elements serve as positive reinforcement, encouraging dogs to repeat desired behaviors and enhancing the bond between pet and owner. However, using these rewards effectively requires an understanding of timing, consistency, and individual preferences.

Every dog is different—some respond eagerly to treats, while others prefer playtime or verbal praise. Finding the right balance and using these rewards correctly ensures that training is both enjoyable and effective. This guide will explore how to use treats, toys, and praise in a structured manner to maximize training success and maintain a well-behaved, happy pet.

Understanding Positive Reinforcement in Training

Positive reinforcement is based on the principle that behaviors followed by a pleasant consequence are more likely to be repeated. When a dog sits and immediately receives a reward, it learns that sitting leads to good things. Over time, the dog will naturally offer the behavior more frequently in anticipation of a reward.

Treats, toys, and praise all serve as reinforcers in different ways:

- Treats provide a food-based reward that is highly motivating for most dogs.
- Toys stimulate a dog's natural desire to play, making training fun.
- Praise offers emotional encouragement and strengthens the human-animal bond.

By incorporating these rewards strategically, trainers can shape behaviors effectively while keeping their dogs engaged and eager to learn.

Using Treats in Training

Why Treats Work

Dogs are naturally food-motivated, making treats one of the easiest and most effective ways to reinforce good behavior. A well-timed treat provides immediate feedback, helping the dog understand which behaviors are desirable.

Choosing the Right Treats

Not all treats are equally effective in training. The right choice depends on the dog's preferences, the training situation, and dietary considerations.

1. High-Value vs. Low-Value Treats:
    - High-value treats (e.g., cheese, chicken, freeze-dried liver) are ideal for challenging training sessions, distractions, and teaching new commands.
    - Low-value treats (e.g., kibble, store-bought biscuits) are best for easy tasks and maintenance training.
2. Small and Soft Treats:
    - Treats should be small enough to be eaten quickly, preventing distractions during training.
    - Soft treats are preferable to crunchy ones since they are easier to consume, allowing for smoother training sessions.
3. Healthy and Nutritious Options:
    - Opt for natural, low-calorie treats to avoid excessive weight gain.
    - Consider using pieces of fruits and vegetables (e.g., carrots, apples) for dogs that enjoy them.

Timing and Consistency

- Immediate Rewarding. The treat must be given immediately after the correct behavior to create a clear association. A delay of even a few seconds can confuse the dog.
- Consistent Use: Until a behavior is well-learned, reward it consistently before gradually reducing treat dependency.

Fading Out Treats Over Time

Once a behavior becomes reliable, treats should be given intermittently rather than every time. This strengthens the behavior while preventing treat dependency. Gradually replace treats with verbal praise, petting, or playtime.

Using Toys as Rewards

Why Toys Can Be Effective

For dogs that love to play, toys can be just as motivating as treats. A well-chosen toy can make training sessions exciting and reinforce desired behaviors through interactive play.

Types of Toy Rewards

Different dogs have different toy preferences, so it's essential to determine what excites each individual pet.

1. Tug Toys: Great for rewarding high-energy behaviors like agility training or impulse control exercises.
2. Fetch Toys (Balls, Frisbees): Ideal for reinforcing recall commands and encouraging focus.
3. Chew Toys: Can be used as a long-term reward after a successful training session.
4. Puzzle Toys: Serve as both mental stimulation and reinforcement, keeping dogs engaged.

When to Use Toys in Training

- Teaching Impulse Control: Asking a dog to sit before throwing a ball reinforces patience.
- Encouraging Engagement: Playtime with a tug toy can serve as a reward after a successful obedience command.
- Training Without Food Dependence: Some dogs may prefer toy rewards over treats, making play an effective training alternative.

Structuring Toy-Based Rewards

- Make the Dog Work for It: Only allow play as a reward for correctly performed behaviors.
- Short Play Sessions: Keep reward playtime brief to maintain focus during training.

- Control the Toy: The toy should not be freely available all the time. Keeping it special makes it more valuable.

Using Praise Effectively

Why Praise is Important

Verbal praise and physical affection strengthen the bond between dog and owner, providing emotional reinforcement alongside tangible rewards. While some dogs are highly food-motivated, others may respond best to praise and attention.

Different Forms of Praise

1. Verbal Praise: Saying "Good dog!" in an enthusiastic tone reinforces positive behavior.
2. Physical Affection: Petting, belly rubs, and gentle pats increase a dog's confidence and reinforce training.
3. Facial Expressions: Smiling and maintaining eye contact show approval and encouragement.

Making Praise More Meaningful

- Use an Excited Tone: Dogs respond well to an enthusiastic, happy voice.
- Pair Praise with Other Rewards: In early training, praise should be combined with treats or toys to strengthen its impact.
- Be Sincere: Dogs can sense insincerity. Genuine praise builds trust and motivation.

Combining Treats, Toys, and Praise for Maximum Effect

The most effective training methods incorporate a mix of treats, toys, and praise, depending on the situation and the dog's preferences. Here's how to balance them:

1. Start with Treats for Learning New Behaviors: Use high-value treats to establish commands and reinforce new training concepts.
2. Introduce Praise and Toys as the Dog Progresses: Once the dog understands the command, start rewarding with praise or a toy intermittently.
3. Gradually Reduce Treats While Increasing Praise: Over time, treats should be used less frequently, while verbal praise and play should become the primary reinforcers.
4. Use Different Rewards for Different Situations:
    - Treats for precision-based commands (e.g., sit, stay, heel).
    - Toys for high-energy commands (e.g., fetch, recall).
    - Praise for reinforcing good manners and daily obedience.

Common Mistakes to Avoid

1. Overfeeding Treats: Giving too many treats can lead to weight gain. Always adjust meal portions accordingly.
2. Inconsistent Rewarding: If some behaviors are rewarded inconsistently, the dog may become confused.
3. Using Treats as Bribes Instead of Rewards: Treats should reinforce behaviors, not lure dogs into obeying only when food is present.
4. Over-Exciting the Dog with Toys: Some dogs become too hyper with toy rewards, making it hard to refocus on training.
5. Ignoring Praise: Relying only on treats can make dogs less responsive when food isn't available.

Using treats, toys, and praise effectively ensures that training remains fun, engaging, and productive. Understanding when and how to use each reward allows trainers to communicate with their dogs clearly and create strong, lasting behaviors.

Overcoming Common Training Challenges

Training a dog can be a rewarding but sometimes frustrating experience. While many dogs respond quickly to basic commands, others may struggle with distractions, stubbornness, or fear-based behaviors. Even well-trained dogs can face setbacks or develop undesirable habits over time. Understanding the root cause of training difficulties and using effective strategies to overcome them is essential for a successful training journey.

Whether you're dealing with a dog that refuses to listen, pulls on the leash, or struggles with recall, there are proven methods to address these challenges.

Understanding Why Training Challenges Occur

Training challenges arise for various reasons, including:

- Lack of Consistency: Dogs need clear, consistent rules and reinforcement. Mixed signals confuse them.
- Distractions: Environments with new smells, people, or other animals can make it hard for a dog to focus.
- Insufficient Motivation: Some dogs require higher-value rewards (e.g., treats, toys, praise) to stay engaged.
- Anxiety or Fear: Fearful dogs may struggle to follow commands due to stress or negative past experiences.
- Overexcitement: Energetic dogs may have trouble concentrating, making training sessions difficult.
- Physical or Medical Issues: Some dogs may be unable to perform certain behaviors due to discomfort or health conditions.

By identifying the underlying cause of training difficulties, dog owners can tailor their approach to effectively address the issue.

Common Training Challenges and How to Overcome Them

1. **Dog Won't Listen or Follow Commands**

One of the most common frustrations in training is a dog that ignores commands. This can happen due to distractions, insufficient training, or a lack of motivation.

Solution:

- Start in a Quiet Environment: Begin training in a distraction-free area before gradually increasing difficulty.
- Use High-Value Rewards: If regular treats aren't working, try using pieces of chicken, cheese, or a favorite toy.
- Ensure Proper Timing: Reward immediately after the correct behavior to reinforce the connection.
- Use Clear and Consistent Cues: Stick to one-word commands (e.g., "sit" instead of "sit down, please").
- Be Patient and Positive: Avoid frustration; dogs learn at their own pace.

2. **Pulling on the Leash**

Many dogs instinctively pull on the leash, making walks challenging and uncomfortable for the owner.

Solution:

- Use a No-Pull Harness: A front-clip harness discourages pulling by redirecting the dog's movement.
- Train the 'Loose-Leash Walking' Command: Reward the dog for walking calmly beside you.
- Stop Moving When Pulling Occurs: The dog will learn that pulling gets them nowhere. Resume walking only when they relax the leash.
- Change Directions Frequently: This keeps the dog focused on you rather than forging ahead.

3. **Jumping on People**

Jumping is a common behavior in excited dogs that want attention. However, it can be problematic, especially for large breeds.

Solution:

- Ignore the Jumping: Turn away and avoid eye contact until the dog is calm, then reward them for sitting.
- Teach an Alternative Behavior: Encourage the dog to sit instead of jump when greeting people.
- Reinforce Calm Behavior: Reward the dog when they remain calm around guests.
- Use a Consistent Approach: Ensure all family members and visitors follow the same rules.

4. **Not Coming When Called (Poor Recall)**

A dog that doesn't come when called can be frustrating and, in some cases, dangerous.

Solution:

- Start in a Controlled Environment: Train recall in a quiet area before progressing to more distracting settings.
- Use High-Value Rewards: Make coming to you more rewarding than any distractions (e.g., treats, playtime).
- Never Punish the Dog for Coming Late: If a dog hesitates but eventually returns, always praise them. Punishing them can create negative associations with recall.
- Practice 'Chase Games': Running away playfully while calling your dog encourages them to follow.

5. **Excessive Barking**

While barking is natural, excessive barking can become a nuisance.

Solution:

- Identify the Trigger: Determine if the barking is due to boredom, anxiety, excitement, or alerting behavior.
- Redirect Attention: Teach a 'quiet' command and reward the dog when they stop barking.
- Provide Mental and Physical Stimulation: Many dogs bark out of boredom, so ensure they receive enough exercise and interactive play.
- Use Controlled Exposure: Gradually expose the dog to triggers at a low intensity and reward calm behavior.

6. **Chewing on Furniture or Household Items**

Dogs chew for various reasons, including teething, boredom, or stress.

Solution:

- Provide Appropriate Chew Toys: Redirect the dog to chew on acceptable items instead of household objects.
- Use Taste Deterrents: Apply bitter sprays to furniture to discourage chewing.
- Increase Exercise and Mental Stimulation: A tired dog is less likely to engage in destructive chewing.
- Crate Training: When unsupervised, keeping the dog in a safe space prevents destructive behavior.

7. Housebreaking Problems

Accidents in the house are common, especially in puppies or newly adopted dogs.

Solution:

- Establish a Regular Schedule: Take the dog outside at consistent times (e.g., after meals, play, and naps).
- Reward Immediately: Praise and treat the dog right after they eliminate outside.
- Supervise and Confine: Use a crate or designated area to prevent accidents when unsupervised.
- Clean Accidents Thoroughly: Use enzyme-based cleaners to remove odors that might attract repeat marking.

8. Fear-Based Reactions or Anxiety

Some dogs react with fear to new people, environments, or situations.

Solution:

- Create Positive Associations: Gradually expose the dog to the fearful stimulus while rewarding calm behavior.
- Avoid Forcing Interactions: Let the dog approach new situations at their own pace.
- Use Calming Aids: Anxiety wraps, pheromone diffusers, or soft music can help relax nervous dogs.
- Work with a Professional: Severe anxiety may require guidance from a behaviorist.

9. Overexcitement and Lack of Focus

Some dogs get overly excited and struggle to concentrate during training.

Solution:

- Exercise Before Training: A short walk or play session can help a dog focus.

- Keep Training Sessions Short: Aim for 5-10 minute sessions to prevent overstimulation.
- Use High-Value Rewards Strategically: Reward calm, focused behavior rather than excitement.
- Incorporate Impulse Control Exercises: Teaching 'wait' and 'stay' commands helps manage excitement.

Final Tips for Overcoming Training Challenges

1. Stay Consistent: Dogs thrive on routine and clear expectations.
2. Be Patient: Every dog learns at their own pace, and setbacks are normal.
3. Use Positive Reinforcement: Rewarding good behavior is more effective than punishing bad behavior.
4. Adapt to Your Dog's Needs: Some dogs need more time, motivation, or different training methods.
5. Seek Professional Help if Needed: If training challenges persist, consulting a dog trainer or behaviorist can provide valuable guidance.

With the right approach, patience, and dedication, even the most challenging training issues can be overcome.

Chapter 4: Leash Training and Off-Leash Control

Leash training and off-leash control are essential for a well-behaved dog. Teaching your dog to walk calmly on a leash and respond reliably off-leash enhances safety, strengthens your bond, and ensures enjoyable walks while preventing pulling, distractions, and wandering.

Choosing the Right Leash, Collar, or Harness for Training

Selecting the right leash, collar, or harness is essential for effective training and ensuring the safety, comfort, and control of your dog. With various options available, understanding the pros and cons of each tool will help you make the best choice for your dog's breed, size, temperament, and training needs.

Before choosing a leash, collar, or harness, it's important to consider:

- Training Goals: Are you teaching basic obedience, leash walking, or off-leash recall?
- Dog's Size and Strength: Large, powerful dogs may require stronger equipment, while smaller dogs need lightweight options.
- Behavioral Issues: Does your dog pull on the leash, jump, or resist walking?
- Comfort and Safety: The right fit prevents discomfort, injuries, or escape attempts.

Once you understand your dog's needs, you can choose the most appropriate training tools.

Choosing the Right Leash

The leash is your primary tool for communication and control during training. There are various types of leashes, each suited for different purposes.

1. Standard Leash

Best for: Everyday walks, basic obedience training.

Features:

- Typically made of nylon, leather, or rope.
- Standard lengths range from 4 to 6 feet.
- Comfortable for both the owner and the dog.

Pros:
✔ Provides good control in normal walking situations.

✔ Durable and easy to handle.
✔ Works well for most dogs.

Cons:
✘ Limited length for training recall or distance commands.
✘ Not ideal for off-leash training.

2. Retractable Leash

Best for: Allowing dogs more freedom while maintaining some control.

Features:

- Extends from 10 to 30 feet with a locking mechanism.
- Usually made of thin cord or tape.

Pros:
✔ Allows dogs to explore while on-leash.
✔ Useful for trained dogs with good recall.

Cons:
✘ Encourages pulling if not used correctly.
✘ Risk of injury if the leash snaps back suddenly.
✘ Not recommended for strong pullers or reactive dogs.

3. Long-Line Leash

Best for: Recall training, off-leash preparation.

Features:

- Can be 15 to 50 feet long.
- Typically made of nylon or rope.

Pros:
✔ Great for teaching recall commands in open areas.
✔ Provides controlled freedom during training.

Cons:
✗ Requires space to use effectively.
✗ Can get tangled if not handled properly.

4. Chain Leash

Best for: Dogs that chew on their leash.

Features:

- Made of metal links.
- Often heavier than standard leashes.

Pros:
✔ Prevents leash chewing.
✔ Very durable.

Cons:
✗ Can be heavy and uncomfortable for both dog and handler.
✗ Not ideal for everyday use.

5. Hands-Free Leash

Best for: Running, hiking, or multi-tasking during walks.

Features:

- Worn around the waist or across the body.
- Made of nylon or bungee material.

Pros:
✔ Allows for hands-free movement.
✔ Good for active owners and jogging.

Cons:
✗ Less control compared to standard leashes.
✗ Not suitable for reactive or strong dogs.

Choosing the Right Collar

Collars serve as a basic attachment point for a leash and an identification tag holder. However, the right collar can also aid in training.

1. Flat Collar

Best for: Everyday wear and ID attachment.

Features:

- Made of nylon, leather, or fabric.
- Comes with a buckle or quick-release clasp.

Pros:
✔ Comfortable for daily wear.
✔ Ideal for dogs that don't pull.

Cons:
✗ Offers minimal training control.
✗ Not suitable for dogs prone to pulling or lunging.

2. Martingale Collar

Best for: Dogs that slip out of standard collars.

Features:

- Tightens slightly when the dog pulls, preventing escape.
- Made of fabric with a limited slip function.

Pros:
✔ Prevents slipping out without choking.
✔ Ideal for breeds with narrow heads (e.g., Greyhounds).

Cons:
✗ Should be used with supervision.
✗ Not ideal for severe pullers.

3. Prong (Pinch) Collar

Best for: Strong, stubborn pullers (used under professional guidance).

Features:

- Metal prongs provide pressure around the neck when the dog pulls.
- Designed to mimic a mother dog's correction.

Pros:
✔ Effective for powerful dogs resistant to other collars.
✔ Provides immediate correction.

Cons:
✘ Must be fitted correctly to prevent injury.
✘ Can be misused and cause harm if not used properly.

4. Head Collar (Halti or Gentle Leader)

Best for: Strong pullers, reactive dogs.

Features:

- Wraps around the muzzle, giving better control of the head.
- Works similarly to a horse's halter.

Pros:
✔ Reduces pulling significantly.
✔ Offers greater control without much force.

Cons:
✘ Some dogs dislike wearing it.
✘ Requires proper introduction and training.

Choosing the Right Harness

Harnesses are an excellent alternative to collars, especially for dogs that pull or have respiratory issues.

1. Back-Clip Harness

Best for: Small dogs or well-trained walkers.

Pros:
✔ Comfortable for most dogs.
✔ Prevents neck strain.

Cons:
✗ Provides less control over pulling.

2. Front-Clip Harness

Best for: Training dogs to stop pulling.

Pros:
✓ Redirects pulling behavior.
✓ Provides better control over movement.

Cons:
✗ Some designs can restrict natural movement.

3. Dual-Clip Harness

Best for: Versatile training needs.

Pros:
✓ Allows both back and front leash attachment.
✓ Provides flexibility for different training stages.

Cons:
✗ Slightly bulkier than single-clip harnesses.

Choosing the right leash, collar, or harness depends on your dog's training stage, size, and behavior.

- For pullers: A front-clip harness or head collar is best.
- For basic training: A standard leash with a flat or martingale collar works well.
- For recall training: A long-line leash is ideal.
- For strong, stubborn dogs: A prong collar (used responsibly) or no-pull harness provides extra control.

Whichever tool you choose, proper introduction, consistent training, and positive reinforcement will ensure a successful and enjoyable training experience for both you and your dog.

Teaching Loose Leash Walking and Preventing Pulling

Loose leash walking is an essential skill for any dog and their owner. It ensures enjoyable, stress-free walks, improves communication, and fosters a strong bond between you and your furry companion. Dogs that pull on the leash not only make walks frustrating but can also risk injury to themselves and their handlers. Teaching your dog to walk politely on a leash requires patience, consistency, and the right techniques.

Before diving into training methods, it's crucial to understand why dogs pull on the leash. Several factors contribute to this behavior:

- Natural Instincts: Dogs are naturally curious and eager to explore their environment. Their keen senses pick up scents, sights, and sounds, making them want to move toward objects of interest.
- Reinforced Behavior: If a dog pulls on the leash and the owner follows by moving in the same direction, the dog learns that pulling gets them where they want to go.
- Excitement and Energy: High-energy breeds or dogs that haven't had enough physical or mental stimulation before a walk may pull due to pent-up energy.
- Lack of Training: Many dogs have never been taught how to walk properly on a leash, leading them to forge ahead without control.

Now that we understand why dogs pull, let's explore how to teach them loose leash walking effectively.

Essential Tools for Loose Leash Walking

The right equipment can make training easier and more effective. Here are some tools to consider:

- Standard 4-6 Foot Leash: Avoid retractable leashes, as they encourage pulling. A standard leash provides better control.
- Front-Clip Harness: Unlike back-clip harnesses, which can encourage pulling, a front-clip harness redirects the dog's movement toward you, making it easier to manage pulling.
- Head Halter: This is useful for strong pullers, as it provides better control over the dog's head movements.
- High-Value Treats: Use small, tasty treats to reinforce good behavior and keep your dog engaged.
- Clicker (Optional): A clicker can help mark the exact moment your dog does something right, reinforcing positive behavior.

Step-by-Step Guide to Teaching Loose Leash Walking

Step 1: Start in a Low-Distraction Environment

Begin training indoors or in your backyard where there are fewer distractions. This allows your dog to focus on learning without the excitement of the outside world.

1. Hold the Leash Correctly: Keep a relaxed grip on the leash, allowing some slack. Avoid keeping the leash too tight, as tension can encourage pulling.
2. Use a Marker Word or Clicker: Choose a word like "yes" or use a clicker to mark correct behavior.

3. Introduce the Heel Position. Have your dog stand next to you (on either your left or right side). Reward them when they remain by your side.

Step 2: Reward for Staying by Your Side

Start walking at a slow pace. Every time your dog walks next to you without pulling, immediately reward them with a treat and praise. Reinforce the idea that staying by your side is rewarding.

- Tip: Hold treats at your side to encourage your dog to stay in the correct position.
- Practice in Short Sessions: Keep initial training sessions between 5 to 10 minutes to avoid overwhelming your dog.

Step 3: Stop Moving When Pulling Occurs

If your dog starts pulling, stop walking immediately. Do not yank the leash or pull them back forcefully. Instead:

1. Stay Still: Wait until your dog stops pulling and returns to a loose leash position.
2. Reward the Correct Position: When they return to your side, give a treat and resume walking.
3. Repeat Consistently: Over time, your dog will learn that pulling does not get them anywhere, while walking calmly leads to movement.

Step 4: Use the "Change Direction" Technique

If your dog frequently pulls forward, try this technique:

1. When Pulling Begins, Change Direction: Instead of stopping, turn around and walk the opposite way.
2. Encourage Your Dog to Follow: Use a happy, encouraging tone and treats to guide them.
3. Reward When They Return to Your Side: Mark the correct behavior with a treat and continue walking.

This method teaches your dog that pulling won't help them reach their desired destination.

Step 5: Introduce the "Leave It" and "Focus" Commands

These commands help redirect your dog's attention when they get distracted.

- Leave It: Teach your dog to ignore distractions (other dogs, squirrels, smells) by rewarding them for disengaging when they hear "leave it."
- Focus: Train your dog to look at you on command, helping them stay attentive during walks.

Step 6: Gradually Increase Distractions

Once your dog masters loose leash walking in a quiet area, gradually expose them to more challenging environments, such as:

- Sidewalks with passing people and bicycles.
- Parks with other dogs and wildlife.
- Busy streets with traffic noises.

Step 7: Reinforce Loose Leash Walking on Every Walk

Consistency is key. Continue reinforcing good walking behavior during every outing. Over time, loose leash walking will become second nature for your dog.

Additional Tips for Preventing Pulling

- Exercise Before Walks: A tired dog is less likely to pull. Play fetch or engage in short training sessions before heading out.
- Keep Walks Enjoyable: Allow your dog some time to explore and sniff within reason. Sniffing is an essential part of their enrichment.
- Use a Firm but Gentle Approach: Avoid harsh corrections or punishments. Instead, focus on rewarding good behavior.
- Set Realistic Expectations: Some dogs take longer to learn loose leash walking, especially strong pullers or young puppies. Patience and consistency will lead to success.

Troubleshooting Common Problems

My Dog Lunges at Other Dogs or People

If your dog gets overly excited or reactive when seeing other dogs or people, work on focus training:

- Increase Distance: Start training from a distance where they can remain calm.
- Use High-Value Treats: Reward calm behavior when they see another dog without reacting.
- Redirect Attention: Use the "focus" command to get them to look at you instead.

My Dog Pulls Towards a Specific Object (e.g., a tree, another dog)

- Use the "Leave It" command to discourage pulling toward distractions.
- Stop walking and only continue once they return to a loose leash position.

My Dog is Easily Distracted on Walks

- Increase mental stimulation before walks (e.g., puzzle toys, short training sessions).
- Start in a familiar, quiet area before progressing to busier locations.

Teaching loose leash walking takes time, but the rewards are worth the effort. A dog that walks politely on a leash is safer, easier to manage, and more enjoyable to take on outings. By using positive reinforcement, patience, and consistent training, you can prevent pulling and turn every walk into a pleasant experience for both you and your dog.

With practice and persistence, you'll soon have a well-mannered walking companion, making your daily strolls an enjoyable bonding time rather than a struggle.

Correcting Lunging, Jumping, and Leash Reactivity

Dogs lunging, jumping, and reacting aggressively on a leash can be challenging behaviors for many dog owners. These behaviors often result from excitement, frustration, fear, or a lack of training. Addressing them requires patience, consistency, and the right techniques to ensure safe and enjoyable walks.

Understanding the Causes of Lunging, Jumping, and Leash Reactivity

Before correcting these behaviors, it's important to understand why they happen.

1. Excitement and Overstimulation

- Some dogs become overly excited when they see people, other dogs, or animals.
- High-energy breeds, young dogs, or under-exercised dogs are more prone to this behavior.

2. Fear or Anxiety

- Some dogs lunge or jump out of fear, using these behaviors as a way to keep threats away.
- Rescue dogs or those with a history of negative experiences may display leash reactivity.

3. Frustration and Barrier Frustration

- A dog that wants to interact but is held back by a leash may become frustrated, leading to lunging and jumping.
- This is common in friendly dogs that are not taught self-control.

4. Lack of Proper Training

- Dogs that have never been taught impulse control often display inappropriate behaviors like lunging and jumping.

- A lack of socialization can lead to overreactions when exposed to new stimuli.

5. Reinforced Behavior

- If lunging or jumping has worked in the past (getting attention, moving forward, or avoiding something), the dog will continue doing it.

Once the cause of the behavior is identified, training can be tailored to address the root issue effectively.

Correcting Lunging Behavior

Lunging is a common issue when dogs encounter other dogs, people, or distractions on walks. It can be triggered by excitement, fear, or frustration.

Step 1: Teach Impulse Control Commands

Impulse control helps dogs remain calm when excited. The following commands should be practiced in low-distraction environments before applying them in real-world situations:

- "Sit" and "Stay" – Reinforces patience and waiting before approaching distractions.
- "Leave It" – Teaches dogs to ignore distractions and focus on their handler.
- "Look at Me" – Encourages eye contact and focus on the handler instead of external stimuli.

Step 2: Use Distance to Prevent Lunging

- If your dog lunges at other dogs or people, start training from a distance where they remain calm.
- Slowly reduce the distance over time as they become more comfortable.

Step 3: Use the "Turn and Redirect" Technique

- When your dog begins to lunge, calmly turn in the opposite direction and walk away.
- Once they calm down, reward them with treats and praise.
- Repeat this technique consistently until they learn that lunging does not get them closer to their target.

Step 4: Reinforce Positive Behavior with Rewards

- Reward calm behavior when encountering triggers.
- Use high-value treats to create positive associations with distractions.

Step 5: Introduce Controlled Socialization

- Slowly expose your dog to triggers in a controlled environment.
- Arrange practice walks with calm, well-behaved dogs to teach proper interactions.

If lunging is due to fear or aggression, consulting a professional trainer or behaviorist may be necessary for additional guidance.

Correcting Jumping Behavior

Jumping is common when dogs are overly excited to greet people. While it may seem harmless, it can be problematic, especially with large dogs or those interacting with children or elderly individuals.

Step 1: Teach an Alternative Greeting Behavior

- Teach your dog to sit when greeting people instead of jumping.
- Ask friends and family to only pet your dog when they remain seated.
- Consistently reinforce this rule so they understand that sitting leads to attention.

Step 2: Ignore the Jumping Behavior

- If your dog jumps on you, turn away and cross your arms.
- Avoid eye contact or verbal interaction.
- Once they calm down, reward them for keeping all four paws on the ground.

Step 3: Use a "Sit to Greet" Routine

- Practice having people approach while your dog sits.
- If they stay seated, allow the person to give them attention.
- If they jump, the person should turn away until the dog sits again.

Step 4: Reinforce Calm Greetings with Positive Reinforcement

- Always reward calm greetings with treats and praise.
- Be consistent, as mixed signals can confuse the dog and prolong the training process.

Step 5: Use a Leash to Control Jumping During Training

- If needed, keep your dog on a leash while training calm greetings.
- Gently step on the leash to prevent excessive movement if they attempt to jump.

Correcting Leash Reactivity

Leash reactivity refers to aggressive or overly excited behavior when a dog encounters other dogs, people, or animals while on a leash. This can include barking, growling, lunging, or snapping.

Step 1: Identify the Trigger and Threshold

- Observe what causes the reaction (dogs, bicycles, joggers, etc.).
- Identify how close the dog must be before reacting (this is their threshold).
- Start training from a distance beyond the threshold and gradually decrease it over time.

Step 2: Use Counter-Conditioning Techniques

- Reward Calm Behavior: When your dog sees a trigger but remains calm, give them a treat.
- Create Positive Associations: Use high-value treats to replace negative emotions with positive experiences.
- Slowly Decrease Distance: As your dog gets better at remaining calm, move closer to the trigger gradually.

Step 3: Teach the "Look at Me" Command

- Before your dog reacts, call their name and reward them for looking at you.
- This redirects their focus and prevents lunging or barking.

Step 4: Use a "U-Turn" to Avoid Reactions

- If your dog starts reacting, calmly turn around and walk in the opposite direction.
- This prevents escalation and teaches them to disengage from the trigger.

Step 5: Manage Walks with Proper Equipment

- Use a front-clip harness or head halter to provide better control.
- Avoid retractable leashes, as they allow too much freedom and increase reactivity risks.

Step 6: Set Up Controlled Exposure Sessions

- Arrange training walks with calm dogs at a safe distance.
- Gradually decrease the distance while reinforcing positive behavior.

General Tips for Long-Term Success

✓ Be Patient and Consistent – Training takes time and must be reinforced daily.
✓ Remain Calm and Confident – Dogs sense their owner's emotions, so avoid tension or frustration.
✓ Provide Mental and Physical Stimulation – A well-exercised dog is less likely to react negatively.

✓ Avoid Punishment-Based Methods – Using corrections like leash jerks or yelling can worsen reactivity.
✓ Use High-Value Rewards – Treats, toys, and praise should be used to reinforce good behavior.

When to Seek Professional Help

If your dog's lunging, jumping, or reactivity becomes severe or leads to aggressive behavior, consulting a professional dog trainer or behaviorist is highly recommended. They can tailor a training program specifically for your dog's needs.

Off-Leash Training: Building Trust and Control in Open Spaces

Off-leash training is one of the most rewarding experiences for both dog owners and their canine companions. It allows dogs to enjoy freedom while ensuring they remain safe, responsive, and under control in open spaces. However, successful off-leash training requires patience, consistency, and proper techniques to build trust and reinforce commands reliably.

The Importance of Off-Leash Training

Off-leash training is not just about giving your dog freedom; it's about ensuring they listen and respond even in the presence of distractions. Some key benefits include:

- Increased Exercise and Mental Stimulation – Dogs can run, explore, and engage in natural behaviors.
- Stronger Bond with Owners – Training builds trust and enhances communication.
- Greater Safety – A well-trained dog is less likely to run into danger or get lost.
- More Enjoyable Walks and Outdoor Adventures – Owners can confidently take their dogs to parks, trails, and open areas.

However, off-leash privileges should only be granted once a dog has demonstrated consistent obedience and impulse control.

Foundational Skills for Off-Leash Training

Before introducing off-leash training, dogs must master essential commands that establish control and reinforce good behavior.

1. Reliable Recall ("Come" Command)

A strong recall is the most important skill for off-leash control. If your dog does not return when called, they should not be off-leash.

How to Train Recall:

- Start in a quiet, enclosed area with minimal distractions.
- Use a happy, inviting tone and call your dog's name followed by "Come!"
- Reward immediately with high-value treats when they respond correctly.
- Gradually increase distance and introduce mild distractions.
- Progress to more challenging environments (parks, trails) only when recall is reliable in controlled settings.

Common Recall Mistakes:

- Scolding the dog when they return – This can make them hesitant to come back.
- Only calling when it's time to leave fun activities – Ensure recall leads to positive experiences.
- Not practicing enough in different environments – Dogs need repetition in various settings to generalize the command.

2. Stay and Wait Commands

A strong stay command prevents dogs from running into unsafe situations and reinforces patience.

Training Steps:

- Start with your dog on a leash. Ask them to sit, then say "Stay."
- Step back gradually, rewarding them for holding position.
- Increase duration and distance while reinforcing with praise and treats.
- Introduce distractions (toys, food, other dogs) and practice in different locations.

3. Focus and Engagement ("Look at Me")

Teaching your dog to make eye contact with you on command ensures they remain attentive off-leash.

Training Steps:

- Hold a treat near your face and say "Look at me" or "Watch."
- Reward immediately when they make eye contact.
- Gradually increase duration and phase out treats over time.

4. Walking Without a Leash ("Heel" Command)

A well-trained off-leash dog should stay close by without pulling ahead or wandering too far.

Training Steps.

- Start on-leash, rewarding your dog for walking beside you.
- Use a verbal cue like "Heel" and reward them for maintaining position.
- Gradually increase distance and introduce off-leash practice in a safe, enclosed space.

Transitioning to Off-Leash Training

Once foundational skills are solid, the next step is transitioning to open spaces.

1. Start in a Safe, Controlled Area

Begin off-leash training in a fenced yard or enclosed dog park where distractions are limited.

- Use a long training leash (30-50 feet) to simulate off-leash freedom while maintaining control.
- Reward your dog for checking in and staying close.
- Gradually increase the distance and level of distractions.

2. Gradually Introduce More Freedom

Once your dog consistently responds to commands in controlled settings, start practicing in larger, semi-enclosed areas such as:

- Quiet nature trails
- Large fenced-in fields
- Empty beaches or meadows

Only allow complete off-leash freedom in areas where it is legally permitted and safe.

3. Use a Training Collar or GPS Tracker (If Needed)

For extra security, consider using:

- GPS tracking collars (e.g., Fi Collar, Garmin) to monitor your dog's location.
- Vibrating or beep training collars (avoid shock collars) for gentle remote communication.

4. Reinforce Check-Ins and Engagement

Encourage your dog to voluntarily check in with you every few minutes by rewarding eye contact, sitting near you, or returning when called.

- Randomly call them back and reward them, then release them again.
- Keep them engaged by playing games like fetch or hide-and-seek.

- If they wander too far, use a recall command and reward them generously.

5. Manage Distractions and Impulse Control

Dogs must learn to resist distractions such as wildlife, other dogs, or unfamiliar people.

Techniques to Improve Focus:

- Practice recall in progressively distracting environments.
- Teach a "Leave It" command to prevent chasing.
- Reward calm behavior when encountering distractions.

Common Challenges and How to Overcome Them

1. Dog Runs Away or Ignores Recall

Solution:

- Increase value of rewards (use chicken, cheese, or a favorite toy).
- Practice in smaller spaces before advancing to open areas.
- Ensure your tone is exciting and positive when calling them.

2. Chasing After Animals or People

Solution:

- Strengthen the "Leave It" command.
- Keep initial off-leash sessions in low-distraction areas.
- Reinforce a strong recall and provide alternative activities (fetch, structured play).

3. Wandering Too Far

Solution:

- Train your dog to naturally stay within a specific radius of you.
- Use a whistle or special cue to signal check-ins.
- Reward them frequently for staying close.

Advanced Off-Leash Skills and Fun Activities

Once your dog has mastered basic off-leash obedience, you can introduce fun and advanced activities.

1. Off-Leash Hiking and Trail Adventures

- Choose dog-friendly trails with minimal distractions.
- Carry a leash for emergencies.
- Ensure your dog stays within sight and responds instantly to commands.

2. Agility and Canine Sports

- Off-leash agility training builds discipline and strengthens trust.
- Activities like flyball, dock diving, and frisbee enhance responsiveness.

3. Scent Work and Tracking Games

- Teach your dog to track scents and find hidden objects.
- Great for mental stimulation and reinforcing recall.

Safety Considerations for Off-Leash Training

1. Choose Safe Environments

- Avoid high-traffic areas, roads, or places with potential hazards.
- Always follow local leash laws and park regulations.

2. Carry Emergency Essentials

- Bring a leash, treats, water, and a pet first-aid kit.
- Have an ID tag and microchip in case your dog gets lost.

3. Be Mindful of Other Dogs and People

- Not all dogs or people are comfortable with off-leash interactions.
- Always call your dog back when approaching others.

Off-leash training is a journey that requires patience, consistency, and trust-building. When done correctly, it enhances the bond between owner and dog while providing safe freedom in open spaces.

Training Reliable Recall: Getting Your Dog to Come Every Time

Reliable recall is one of the most important skills a dog can learn. It ensures your dog's safety, gives them more freedom, and strengthens your bond. However, recall training is also one of the most challenging obedience skills because dogs are naturally curious and easily distracted.

Why Recall Training Is Essential

A strong recall command is crucial for several reasons:

- Safety – Prevents your dog from running into traffic, encountering aggressive animals, or getting lost.
- Freedom – A dog with reliable recall can enjoy off-leash time at parks, trails, and beaches.
- Better Behavior – A well-trained dog that responds to recall is easier to manage in social situations.
- Stronger Bond – Recall training builds trust and enhances communication between you and your dog.

However, reliable recall isn't something that happens overnight. It requires consistency, patience, and positive reinforcement.

Step 1: Choosing a Recall Cue

Your recall cue should be clear, distinct, and consistent. Some common recall cues include:

- "Come!" – The most widely used recall command.
- Whistle recall – A high-pitched sound that carries further than a voice.
- Unique words (e.g., "Here!" or "To Me!") – Useful if "Come" has been overused or ignored.

Tips for Choosing a Recall Cue:

✅ Use a cue that is not used in everyday conversation to avoid confusion.
✅ Say the cue in a happy, inviting tone to encourage your dog to come.
✅ Keep it consistent—don't switch between different words.

Step 2: Building a Strong Foundation Indoors

Before expecting your dog to come in a park or a distracting outdoor setting, train in a controlled, low-distraction environment like your home.

Training Steps:

1. Start with Short Distances
    - Get your dog's attention by calling their name.
    - Say your recall cue (e.g., "Come!") in an excited, happy tone.
    - Encourage movement by crouching down, clapping, or running backward.
    - Reward them immediately with high-value treats when they reach you.
2. Increase the Distance
    - Gradually call from farther away within the house.
    - Reward every time they respond correctly.

3. Use a Leash for Control
   - Attach a leash to gently guide them toward you if they hesitate.
   - Praise and reward as soon as they start moving in your direction.
4. Practice in Different Rooms
   - Changing locations prevents the dog from associating recall only with one specific place.

Pro Tip:

🏆 Use high-value rewards (chicken, cheese, freeze-dried liver) to make recall exciting.
🏆 Never scold your dog for coming late. Always make recall a positive experience!

Step 3: Transitioning to Outdoor Training

Once your dog reliably responds indoors, start practicing in a more distracting environment like your backyard or a quiet park.

Training Steps:

1. Use a Long Leash for Safety
   - A long training leash (15-50 feet) allows freedom while maintaining control.
   - Call your dog and gently guide them in if they don't respond immediately.
2. Increase the Level of Distractions
   - Start with mild distractions (toys, treats, mild noises).
   - Progress to more challenging ones (other dogs, squirrels, moving cars).
3. Make Coming to You More Rewarding Than Exploring
   - Use a jackpot reward (a handful of treats) for extra distractions.
   - Play with them when they return (tug, fetch, or a belly rub).
4. Practice Frequently
   - Aim for multiple short recall sessions daily rather than long ones.

Common Mistakes to Avoid:

✘ Calling your dog only when playtime ends (they'll learn to avoid coming).
✘ Using a harsh tone or punishment for slow responses.
✘ Repeating the recall command multiple times—say it once and wait.

Step 4: Off-Leash Recall Training

Once your dog consistently responds to recall on a long leash, it's time to transition to off-leash training in a secure area.

Training Steps:

1. Start in a Fenced Area
   - Practice recall in a fully enclosed space where they can't run away.
2. Introduce Freedom Gradually
   - If your dog responds well, allow them short bursts of off-leash time before recalling them.
   - Always reward generously when they return.
3. Practice with Increasing Distance
   - Call them from greater distances and in different locations.
   - If they hesitate, use a happy voice, movement, or a favorite toy to encourage them.
4. Test with More Distractions
   - Add other dogs, wildlife, or moving objects into training environments.
   - Reward highly for coming back despite distractions.
5. Use a Recall Game
   - Play recall games like "Hide and Seek" to reinforce the behavior in a fun way.

Advanced Recall Training: Proofing in High-Distraction Environments

Even if your dog recalls well in a controlled setting, real-life distractions can cause them to ignore you. Proofing recallensures they respond anywhere, anytime.

How to Proof Recall:

✔ Train in multiple environments (parks, beaches, hiking trails).
✔ Increase distraction levels gradually (start with mild distractions before exposing them to high-stimulation areas).
✔ Practice at different times of the day to help them generalize the behavior.
✔ Use real-world distractions—call your dog back from playing with other dogs, sniffing, or chasing.
✔ Reinforce recall randomly—sometimes call them just to give a treat and let them go again.

Emergency Recall: A Lifesaving Skill

An emergency recall is a special supercharged recall cue used only in high-risk situations.

How to Train Emergency Recall:

- Choose a unique word (e.g., "Now!" or a whistle).
- Use only high-value rewards (cheese, steak, or a favorite toy).
- Train in a calm environment first, then introduce distractions.
- Only use the emergency recall for true emergencies to keep it reliable.

Common Recall Training Problems & Solutions

● Dog Ignores Recall in High-Distraction Areas
☑ Go back to practicing in lower-distraction areas and build up gradually.
☑ Use higher-value treats and exciting reinforcement.

● Dog Comes but Stops a Few Feet Away
☑ Use a treat magnet (hold a treat at their nose and lure them in).
☑ Reward only when they fully reach you.

● Dog Runs Away After Recall
☑ Avoid grabbing their collar aggressively when they return.
☑ Reward, pet, and release them occasionally to avoid associating recall with losing freedom.

Training reliable recall is an ongoing process that requires reinforcement throughout your dog's life. Here's how to keep recall strong:

✔ Practice regularly – Even after mastering recall, reinforce it weekly.
✔ Always make recall positive – Never use recall for punishment.
✔ Use recall in everyday life – Call them for meals, playtime, and affection.
✔ Be patient – Some dogs take longer than others, but consistency will pay off.

By investing time in recall training, you'll create a safer, happier, and more well-behaved dog that you can confidently enjoy off-leash adventures with! 🐾

Chapter 5: Behavioral Training and Problem-Solving

Training a well-behaved dog goes beyond teaching basic obedience commands. It involves understanding canine behavior, identifying problem behaviors, and using the right training methods to correct them effectively. Whether you are dealing with excessive barking, jumping, leash pulling, aggression, or separation anxiety, the key to behavioral training lies in patience, consistency, and positive reinforcement.

Before addressing behavioral problems, it is essential to understand why dogs behave the way they do. Dogs communicate through body language, vocalizations, and learned behaviors. Many undesirable behaviors stem from fear, anxiety, lack of training, boredom, or natural instincts.

Key Factors That Influence Behavior:

- ☑ Genetics – Some behaviors are breed-specific (e.g., herding, digging, guarding).
- ☑ Early Socialization – Poorly socialized dogs may develop fear or aggression.
- ☑ Training History – Dogs who haven't been properly trained may develop bad habits.
- ☑ Environment – Changes in routine, household dynamics, or lack of mental stimulation can affect behavior.
- ☑ Medical Issues – Health problems, including pain, thyroid issues, or hearing loss, can cause behavioral changes.

Understanding these influences will help tailor an effective training plan for your dog.

Addressing Common Behavioral Problems

1. Excessive Barking

Dogs bark for various reasons—alerting, boredom, excitement, anxiety, or attention-seeking. While barking is a natural behavior, excessive barking can become problematic.

Training Solutions:

✓ Identify the trigger – Observe when and why your dog barks.
✓ Teach the "Quiet" command – Say "Quiet" in a calm voice and reward silence.
✓ Ignore attention-seeking barking – Reward your dog only when they stop barking.
✓ Provide mental and physical exercise – A tired dog is less likely to bark excessively.
✓ Use desensitization techniques – If your dog barks at strangers, gradually expose them to controlled social situations.

What to Avoid:

✘ Yelling—it encourages more barking.

✘ Using punishment—it can increase anxiety-driven barking.

2. Jumping on People

Dogs jump as a way of greeting or seeking attention. While this may seem harmless, it can be dangerous for children or elderly individuals.

Training Solutions:

✓ Ignore jumping – Turn away and give attention only when your dog has all four paws on the ground.

✓ Teach the "Sit" command – Reward your dog for sitting instead of jumping.

✓ Use the "Off" command – Gently redirect them off and reward calm behavior.

✓ Manage excitement levels – Teach your dog to stay calm when guests arrive.

What to Avoid:

✘ Pushing your dog away—it may encourage jumping as a game.

✘ Kneeling or petting while they jump—it reinforces the behavior.

3. Leash Pulling

Dogs pull on the leash out of excitement or to explore their environment. Teaching loose leash walking requires consistency and practice.

Training Solutions:

✓ Use a no-pull harness – Helps discourage pulling without discomfort.

✓ Stop moving when pulling starts – Only move forward when the leash is loose.

✓ Reward walking by your side – Use treats to encourage a loose leash.

✓ Change direction frequently – This keeps your dog focused on you.

What to Avoid:

✘ Pulling back on the leash—it may cause resistance and worsen pulling.

✘ Using choke or prong collars—they can cause physical harm and fear-based behavior.

4. Aggression and Reactivity

Aggression can be fear-based, territorial, protective, or resource-guarding. If your dog exhibits aggressive behavior, it's crucial to address it immediately.

Training Solutions:

✔ Identify triggers – Observe what causes aggression (e.g., strangers, other dogs).
✔ Use positive reinforcement – Reward calm behavior instead of punishing aggression.
✔ Practice controlled socialization – Gradually expose your dog to triggers at a safe distance.
✔ Teach the "Leave It" and "Look at Me" commands – Redirect focus from triggers.
✔ Seek professional help if needed – Severe aggression may require a behaviorist.

What to Avoid:

✘ Punishing aggression—it can increase fear and worsen behavior.
✘ Forcing interactions—it may escalate aggressive reactions.

5. Separation Anxiety

Dogs with separation anxiety may show destructive behavior, excessive whining, or attempts to escape when left alone.

Training Solutions:

✔ Gradually increase alone time – Start with short periods and slowly extend.
✔ Create a positive departure routine – Give a treat-filled toy before leaving.
✔ Practice calm arrivals and departures – Avoid making a big deal out of leaving.
✔ Provide mental stimulation – Puzzle toys and interactive feeders help keep them occupied.

What to Avoid:

✘ Comforting excessive anxiety—it reinforces the fear.
✘ Punishing destructive behavior—it increases stress and anxiety.

6. Digging

Some breeds (like terriers) have a natural instinct to dig. However, excessive digging can be problematic.

Training Solutions:

✔ Provide a designated digging area – A sandbox or soft dirt patch can help.
✔ Ensure adequate exercise – Digging is often a sign of boredom.
✔ Use deterrents in unwanted areas – Rocks, citrus peels, or motion-activated devices can help.

What to Avoid:

✘ Scolding after the fact—your dog won't understand why they're being punished.

7. Food Aggression and Resource Guarding

Some dogs growl or snap when someone approaches their food or toys.

Training Solutions:

✓ Hand-feed meals – This builds trust and reduces guarding instincts.
✓ Practice trading games – Offer a treat in exchange for a toy or food item.
✓ Teach the "Drop It" command – Reward voluntary item release.

What to Avoid:
✗ Taking items by force—it reinforces defensive behavior.

The Power of Consistency and Positive Reinforcement

Behavioral training is an ongoing process that requires patience and repetition. The best results come from using positive reinforcement methods, where desirable behaviors are rewarded, and unwanted behaviors are redirected.

Key Training Principles:

☑ Timing is critical – Reward within seconds of good behavior.
☑ Use high-value rewards – Treats, praise, or play depending on what motivates your dog.
☑ Be consistent – Ensure all family members follow the same rules.
☑ Avoid punishment-based training – Fear-based techniques can create long-term behavioral issues.

When to Seek Professional Help

If your dog's behavior is severe, dangerous, or does not improve despite training, consult a certified dog trainer, veterinary behaviorist, or animal behavior expert. Some behaviors may be linked to medical issues, so a vet check-up is recommended.

Training is a lifelong journey, not a one-time event. Understanding your dog's needs, communicating clearly, and using humane training techniques will result in a well-behaved, happy, and confident companion.

How to Stop Excessive Barking

Barking is a natural behavior for dogs—they bark to communicate, express emotions, warn of danger, and sometimes simply out of excitement. However, excessive barking can become a problem, especially when it disrupts your home, your neighbors, or your daily life. Learning how to manage and reduce unnecessary barking is essential for a peaceful household.

Before you can effectively stop excessive barking, it's important to understand why your dog is barking. Dogs don't bark just to be annoying; they bark because they are trying to communicate something.

Common Reasons for Barking:

☑ Alert Barking – Dogs bark to warn their owners about unfamiliar sights, sounds, or people. This is common in territorial or protective breeds.

☑ Attention-Seeking Barking – Some dogs bark to get their owner's attention, especially if they have learned that barking results in play, treats, or petting.

☑ Boredom or Loneliness – Dogs that lack mental or physical stimulation may bark excessively out of frustration or boredom.

☑ Separation Anxiety – Dogs experiencing distress when left alone may bark excessively as part of their anxiety.

☑ Frustration Barking – If a dog wants something but can't get it (e.g., being confined, seeing another dog but not being able to approach), they may bark out of frustration.

☑ Playful or Excited Barking – Some dogs bark when playing, especially when chasing toys, other pets, or engaging in rough play.

☑ Fear or Anxiety – Barking can be a response to fear, such as loud noises (thunder, fireworks) or new environments.

☑ Medical Issues – Some dogs bark due to health problems, pain, or cognitive dysfunction in senior dogs.

Understanding the root cause of barking will help determine the best training approach.

Step-by-Step Training to Reduce Excessive Barking

1. Identify the Barking Triggers

The first step in solving excessive barking is identifying when, where, and why your dog is barking.

📌 **Keep a Barking Log:**

- What time does the barking happen?
- What is happening around your dog?
- Is there a specific person, object, or noise causing the barking?
- What is your dog's body language during barking? (Excited, fearful, tense?)

Once you recognize the pattern, you can address the root cause effectively.

2. Remove or Reduce Exposure to Triggers

If your dog barks at specific triggers (e.g., other dogs, passing cars, mail carriers), the simplest solution is to minimize their exposure.

☑ Block Visual Triggers – Close curtains, use window film, or move furniture to prevent your dog from seeing outside distractions.
☑ Reduce Noise Sensitivity – Use white noise machines or calming music to mask outside sounds.
☑ Limit Access to Barking Zones – If your dog barks at the front door, keep them in another room during high-traffic hours.

However, avoidance alone is not a complete solution. You need to train alternative behaviors.

3. Teach the "Quiet" Command

Training your dog to understand the "Quiet" command will help control barking on cue.

◆ Step 1: Allow Your Dog to Bark – Wait for them to start barking naturally at a trigger.
◆ Step 2: Say "Quiet" in a Calm, Firm Voice – Avoid yelling, as it may make your dog bark more.
◆ Step 3: Reward Silence – The moment your dog stops barking, praise them and give a treat.
◆ Step 4: Gradually Increase the Time Before Rewarding – Start by rewarding after a few seconds of silence, then increase to 10–15 seconds.

💡 Pro Tip: If your dog struggles to stop barking, use a distraction like a treat or toy to redirect their focus.

4. Ignore Attention-Seeking Barking

If your dog barks to get attention, don't reward the behavior by giving in.

✔ Turn your back or walk away when they bark for attention.
✔ Reward only quiet behavior – Once they stop barking, give them attention or a treat.
✔ Stay consistent – If you occasionally respond to barking, your dog will learn that barking works.

✘ *What to Avoid:*

- Never yell at your dog—it sounds like barking back to them and can make the behavior worse.
- Don't physically punish your dog—this can increase anxiety and fear-based barking.

5. Provide Enough Physical and Mental Exercise

Many dogs bark because they have pent-up energy. A tired dog is a quiet dog!

☑ Daily Walks & Exercise – Regular physical activity prevents boredom barking.
☑ Puzzle Toys & Mental Stimulation – Keep your dog's mind engaged with treat-dispensing toys or training games.
☑ Obedience Training – Teaching new tricks and reinforcing commands keeps your dog mentally focused.
☑ Playtime – Interactive play with toys or fetch helps release excess energy.

💡 Pro Tip: Certain breeds, like Border Collies and Huskies, need more mental and physical stimulation than others.

6. Desensitize Your Dog to Barking Triggers

If your dog barks at specific stimuli (e.g., doorbells, other dogs, strangers), use desensitization training.

◆ Step 1: Expose Your Dog to the Trigger at a Distance – Keep the trigger at a distance where your dog notices it but doesn't bark.
◆ Step 2: Reward Calm Behavior – Give treats and praise when they stay quiet.
◆ Step 3: Gradually Move Closer – Reduce the distance over time while reinforcing calm behavior.
◆ Step 4: Pair the Trigger with a Positive Association – Teach your dog that the trigger leads to good things (treats, praise, play).

7. Train an Alternative Behavior

Instead of barking, teach your dog to respond to triggers with a different behavior.

✔ "Go to Your Spot" Command – Train your dog to go to a designated area instead of barking at the door.
✔ "Fetch a Toy" Routine – When excited, have your dog grab a toy instead of barking.
✔ "Sit and Stay" Training – Reward your dog for calmly sitting instead of barking.

These alternative behaviors help redirect energy into positive actions rather than barking.

When to Seek Professional Help

If your dog's barking is severe, persistent, or linked to aggression or extreme anxiety, a professional dog trainer or behaviorist can help.

✒ *Consider professional help if:*

- Your dog's barking is uncontrollable despite training efforts.
- The barking is linked to separation anxiety or fear aggression.
- You need guidance on more advanced training techniques.

Stopping excessive barking does not mean silencing your dog completely—it means teaching them when and where barking is appropriate. With patience, consistency, and the right training methods, you can reduce unnecessary barking while maintaining a healthy and communicative relationship with your dog.

Dealing with Aggression: Causes and Solutions

Aggression is a complex behavior that can manifest in various ways across different species, including humans and animals. It is often misunderstood, leading to mismanagement and negative consequences. Understanding the underlying causes of aggression and implementing effective solutions is essential for fostering a harmonious environment, whether in homes, workplaces, or pet care. This comprehensive guide explores the different causes of aggression and provides practical solutions to manage and mitigate aggressive behavior.

Aggression is a behavioral response that can be either instinctual or learned. It is often triggered by various internal and external factors, including genetics, environment, past experiences, and social dynamics. Aggression can be categorized into different types, each requiring a specific approach to management and resolution.

Types of Aggression

- Defensive Aggression
    - Occurs when an individual or animal perceives a threat and reacts to protect themselves.
    - Common in situations where one feels cornered or trapped.
- Territorial Aggression
    - Involves defending a specific space or resource, such as home, workplace, or feeding area.
    - Common in pets, especially dogs, when they guard their homes.
- Fear-Based Aggression
    - Triggered by fear or past trauma.
    - Can be unpredictable and difficult to manage without proper intervention.
- Frustration-Induced Aggression

- o Arises when an individual is unable to achieve a desired outcome or goal.
  - o Common in both humans and animals when restrained or restricted.
- Social Aggression
  - o Related to dominance and hierarchical structures.
  - o Often seen in pack animals, workplaces, and social groups.
- Pain-Induced Aggression
  - o Occurs when an individual or animal is experiencing pain and reacts aggressively as a defensive mechanism.
- Maternal Aggression
  - o Found in mothers protecting their offspring.
  - o Common in both humans and animals as a natural instinct.
- Predatory Aggression
  - o Involves hunting or stalking behavior.
  - o Different from defensive aggression as it is often silent and calculated.

Causes of Aggression

Understanding the root cause of aggression is crucial for implementing effective solutions. Below are some primary factors that contribute to aggressive behavior.

Biological and Genetic Factors

- Some individuals and animal breeds are genetically predisposed to aggressive behavior.
- Hormonal imbalances, such as high testosterone levels, can contribute to aggression.
- Neurological disorders or brain injuries may cause sudden aggressive outbursts.

Environmental Influences

- A stressful or hostile environment can lead to aggressive behavior.
- Lack of proper socialization during early stages of life can make animals and humans more aggressive.
- Exposure to violence or aggressive role models reinforces aggressive tendencies.

Past Trauma and Negative Experiences

- Abuse, neglect, or mistreatment can lead to fear-based aggression.
- Post-Traumatic Stress Disorder (PTSD) in both humans and animals can cause defensive aggression.

Lack of Training and Discipline

- Inadequate training can lead to poor impulse control and aggression.

- Inconsistent rules and boundaries may cause frustration and territorial aggression.

Medical Conditions and Pain

- Conditions such as arthritis, dental pain, or infections can cause irritability and aggression.
- Neurological disorders like rabies in animals or mental health disorders in humans can result in aggression.

Resource Guarding and Competition

- Competition over food, toys, or personal space can lead to aggressive encounters.
- Workplace aggression often stems from competition for promotions, recognition, or control.

Solutions for Managing Aggression

Managing aggression requires a combination of training, behavioral therapy, medical intervention, and environmental modifications. Below are effective strategies to prevent and control aggressive behavior.

Behavioral Training and Socialization

- Early socialization helps individuals and animals develop positive interactions.
- Positive reinforcement training discourages aggressive responses and promotes good behavior.
- Desensitization techniques help reduce fear-based aggression by gradually exposing the individual to the trigger in a controlled manner.

Creating a Safe and Calm Environment

- Reducing stressors in the environment minimizes aggressive responses.
- Establishing clear boundaries and consistent routines prevents frustration-induced aggression.
- Providing a designated safe space for relaxation helps in calming anxious individuals and animals.

Addressing Medical Conditions

- Regular health checkups help diagnose and treat underlying medical causes of aggression.
- Pain management strategies, such as medication or therapy, reduce pain-induced aggression.

Using Positive Reinforcement

- Rewarding good behavior encourages non-aggressive responses.
- Avoiding punishment-based training prevents fear-based aggression from escalating.

Managing Resource Guarding

- Teaching individuals and animals to share through controlled exercises reduces territorial aggression.
- Providing multiple resources (food bowls, toys, personal space) prevents competition-driven aggression.

Professional Intervention and Therapy

- Consulting a behavioral therapist or animal trainer provides expert guidance.
- Cognitive-behavioral therapy (CBT) helps individuals manage anger and frustration effectively.
- Medication, such as anti-anxiety drugs, may be prescribed in severe cases.

Conflict Resolution Techniques

- Open communication and mediation reduce aggression in workplace or social settings.
- Encouraging empathy and understanding helps defuse tense situations.
- Implementing anger management strategies, such as breathing exercises and mindfulness, reduces impulsive aggression.

Preventing Aggressive Behavior

Prevention is always better than intervention when it comes to aggression. Implementing preventive measures helps reduce the likelihood of aggressive outbursts.

For Humans

- Develop emotional intelligence and self-control techniques.
- Practice stress management through relaxation exercises and physical activity.
- Maintain healthy relationships with clear boundaries and respectful communication.

For Pets and Animals

- Begin socialization and training at an early age.
- Provide mental and physical stimulation to prevent boredom-induced aggression.
- Monitor interactions with other pets and humans to prevent conflicts.

Aggression, while a natural response in certain situations, can be managed and controlled through proper understanding and intervention. Identifying the underlying causes of aggression is the first step in finding a suitable solution. Whether dealing with aggression in pets, workplace environments, or personal relationships, a combination of training, therapy, medical care, and preventive strategies can lead to long-term success.

Separation Anxiety: Prevention and Treatment

Separation anxiety is a condition that affects both humans and animals, causing distress when separated from a loved one or caregiver. It is especially common in pets, particularly dogs and cats, but can also be seen in children and even adults. This emotional response is driven by fear, insecurity, and attachment issues, leading to destructive behavior, excessive vocalization, and severe stress.

Understanding separation anxiety, its causes, symptoms, and effective treatment methods is crucial in fostering a healthy and independent mindset, whether in pets or people.

Separation anxiety occurs when an individual or animal becomes overly dependent on another for emotional security. The anxiety manifests when they are left alone, leading to panic, destructive behavior, excessive vocalization, and attempts to escape.

Common Signs of Separation Anxiety

- Excessive Vocalization
    - Continuous barking, whining, meowing, or crying when left alone.
- Destructive Behavior
    - Chewing furniture, scratching doors, tearing objects, or digging in an attempt to escape.
- House Soiling
    - Urination or defecation indoors, despite being house-trained.
- Pacing and Restlessness
    - Walking in circles, pacing back and forth, or constant agitation when alone.
- Refusal to Eat or Drink
    - Loss of appetite when the attachment figure is absent.
- Excessive Salivation and Panting
    - Drooling excessively or breathing heavily due to stress.
- Self-Harm
    - Biting, licking, or chewing themselves excessively, leading to sores or hair loss.
- Depressive Symptoms
    - Lethargy, withdrawal, or lack of interest in play and activities when alone.

Causes of Separation Anxiety

Several factors contribute to separation anxiety, making some individuals more prone to it than others. Understanding these causes can help in designing an effective prevention and treatment plan.

Early Life Experiences

- Orphaned, abandoned, or rehomed pets are more susceptible to separation anxiety.

95

- Children raised in insecure environments or with excessive dependency on caregivers may develop attachment-related anxiety.

Changes in Routine

- Sudden changes, such as moving to a new home, schedule shifts, or changes in caregivers, can trigger anxiety.
- Pets who experience a sudden increase in time spent alone may struggle with adaptation.

Over-Attachment and Dependency

- Constant companionship without fostering independence leads to dependency issues.
- Lack of confidence in being alone increases the likelihood of separation anxiety.

Previous Trauma or Neglect

- Individuals and pets who have experienced abuse or prolonged isolation often develop anxiety.
- Rescued or adopted pets are more prone to developing attachment disorders.

Genetic Predisposition

- Certain breeds of dogs and cats are more prone to separation anxiety due to their social nature.
- Some individuals have a natural predisposition to heightened anxiety and stress responses.

Prevention of Separation Anxiety

Preventing separation anxiety is easier than treating it. Establishing healthy habits and routines from an early stage helps individuals and pets develop independence and confidence.

Encouraging Independence

- Gradually increase the time spent alone to build confidence in solitude.
- Provide engaging activities and mental stimulation to prevent boredom.
- Avoid excessive attachment behaviors, such as constant carrying or following.

Establishing a Secure Routine

- Create a consistent daily schedule that includes feeding, exercise, and alone time.
- Maintain predictable departures and arrivals to reduce anxiety triggers.

Practicing Short Absences

- Start with brief departures and gradually extend the duration.
- Use positive reinforcement, such as treats or praise, upon returning.

Providing Comfort and Distractions

- Leave comforting items, such as blankets or clothing with familiar scents.
- Offer interactive toys, puzzle feeders, or calming music to create a soothing environment.

Socialization and Exposure Training

- Expose pets and individuals to various environments, people, and experiences to build confidence.
- Encourage interactions with other animals and humans to reduce excessive reliance on one individual.

Treatment of Separation Anxiety

Once separation anxiety develops, treatment requires patience, consistency, and a combination of behavioral training and supportive care.

Desensitization and Counterconditioning

- Gradually expose the individual or pet to being alone in a controlled manner.
- Associate alone time with positive experiences, such as treats, toys, or enjoyable activities.
- Reduce the significance of departures by avoiding emotional farewells and greetings.

Behavior Modification Techniques

- Ignore attention-seeking behaviors to reduce dependency.
- Reward calm and independent behavior with positive reinforcement.
- Practice "sit and stay" exercises to build patience and confidence.

Environmental Adjustments

- Provide a comfortable and secure space with familiar objects.
- Use calming aids such as pheromone diffusers, anxiety wraps, or herbal supplements.
- Keep the home environment enriched with interactive toys and mental stimulation.

Training Through Simulated Departures

- Pretend to leave by grabbing keys or putting on shoes, then staying home to reduce departure anxiety.
- Step outside for a few minutes and gradually extend the time spent away.

Engaging in Physical and Mental Exercise

- Increase physical activities such as walks, playtime, or training sessions before departures.
- Mental stimulation through puzzle toys, scent games, or obedience training helps reduce stress.

Medication and Professional Help

- In severe cases, anti-anxiety medications or natural calming supplements may be recommended.
- Consult a behaviorist or veterinarian for personalized treatment plans.
- Cognitive-behavioral therapy (CBT) can help individuals struggling with separation anxiety.

Helping Pets with Separation Anxiety

Since pets rely on their owners for emotional support, separation anxiety can be particularly distressing for them. Special care and structured training can help alleviate their distress.

Crate Training and Safe Spaces

- Introduce crate training as a positive and safe experience rather than confinement.
- Designate a cozy space with soft bedding, toys, and familiar scents.

Using Technology to Provide Comfort

- Use pet cameras with two-way audio to interact with pets when away.
- Automatic treat dispensers or interactive toys help keep pets engaged.

Hiring Pet Sitters or Daycare Services

- Consider pet daycare services for highly social pets.
- Hire a trusted pet sitter or neighbor for companionship during long absences.

Practicing Calm Departures and Arrivals

- Avoid making leaving and returning a dramatic event.
- Wait until the pet is calm before greeting them to prevent reinforcing anxious behavior.

Helping Humans with Separation Anxiety

Separation anxiety is not limited to pets—humans can also suffer from it, especially children and individuals with attachment issues. Practical steps can help in managing and overcoming this anxiety.

Building Emotional Resilience

- Develop self-confidence and coping mechanisms through therapy or self-help techniques.
- Engage in hobbies and activities to shift focus from anxious thoughts.

Establishing Boundaries and Independence

- Encourage personal space and self-sufficiency in relationships.
- Avoid excessive reliance on a single person for emotional stability.

Seeking Therapy and Support

- Cognitive-behavioral therapy (CBT) helps in addressing underlying fears and insecurities.
- Support groups and counseling provide reassurance and coping strategies.

Gradual Exposure to Separation

- Start with small periods of separation and gradually increase the time apart.
- Engage in activities that reinforce independence and reduce attachment dependence.

Separation anxiety, though distressing, is manageable with the right approach. Understanding the causes and symptoms allows for early intervention and effective treatment. Whether dealing with pets or humans, fostering independence, providing environmental enrichment, and using behavioral modification techniques can significantly reduce anxiety.

Destructive Chewing and Resource Guarding

Destructive chewing and resource guarding are two of the most common behavioral issues in pets, particularly in dogs and cats. While chewing is a natural behavior that helps animals explore their environment, relieve stress, and maintain dental health, it becomes problematic when directed toward inappropriate objects. Similarly, resource guarding is a deeply ingrained survival instinct, but it can lead to aggressive and possessive behavior if not managed properly.

Understanding the causes, prevention methods, and effective solutions for these behaviors is essential in ensuring a balanced and harmonious relationship with pets. This guide provides an in-depth exploration of destructive chewing and resource guarding, along with practical steps for prevention and treatment.

Destructive Chewing

Understanding Destructive Chewing

Chewing is a natural and necessary behavior for pets. It helps maintain oral health, alleviates boredom, and provides comfort. However, when chewing is directed toward furniture, clothing, shoes, or other valuable household items, it becomes destructive and frustrating for pet owners.

Causes of Destructive Chewing

- **Teething in Puppies and Kittens**
    - Young animals chew to soothe sore gums during teething.
- **Boredom and Lack of Stimulation**
    - Pets left alone for long periods without mental or physical stimulation resort to chewing as a coping mechanism.
- **Anxiety and Stress**
    - Separation anxiety, changes in routine, or unfamiliar environments can lead to stress-induced chewing.
- **Hunger or Nutritional Deficiencies**
    - Pets on an inadequate diet may chew on non-food objects to satisfy hunger or mineral cravings.
- **Attention-Seeking Behavior**
    - Some pets chew on household items to get a reaction from their owners, whether positive or negative.
- **Lack of Training and Boundaries**
    - Without proper training, pets do not understand which objects are acceptable to chew.
- **Instinctual Behavior**
    - Dogs and cats use their mouths to explore their surroundings, which can sometimes lead to inappropriate chewing.

Prevention and Management of Destructive Chewing

- **Providing Appropriate Chewing Alternatives**
    - Offer a variety of chew toys, bones, and interactive play items that satisfy chewing instincts.
    - Rotate toys regularly to keep them interesting and engaging.
- **Mental and Physical Stimulation**
    - Increase exercise and playtime to prevent boredom-induced chewing.
    - Use puzzle feeders and treat-dispensing toys for mental enrichment.
- **Training and Positive Reinforcement**
    - Redirect pets to appropriate chewing items and reward them when they use them.
    - Discourage chewing on household items with firm but calm corrections.
- **Using Deterrents**
    - Apply bitter sprays or safe deterrents on furniture, shoes, or other commonly chewed items.
    - Provide acceptable alternatives alongside deterrents to encourage proper choices.

- Managing the Environment
    - Keep valuable or dangerous objects out of reach.
    - Crate training or using a pet-safe area when unsupervised can prevent destructive chewing.
- Addressing Anxiety-Related Chewing
    - Establish a consistent routine to reduce stress and anxiety.
    - Use calming pheromone diffusers or anxiety wraps to soothe anxious pets.

Resource Guarding

Understanding Resource Guarding

Resource guarding occurs when a pet becomes overly possessive of food, toys, treats, bedding, or even their human companions. It is a natural survival instinct but can escalate into aggressive behavior, including growling, snapping, or biting when someone approaches their possessions.

Common Signs of Resource Guarding

- Growling, Snarling, or Snapping
    - Defensive behavior when someone approaches their food, toys, or space.
- Rigid Body Language and Staring
    - Freezing or intense focus when guarding a valued resource.
- Eating Faster When Approached
    - Some pets will gulp down food quickly to prevent it from being taken away.
- Blocking Access to an Object
    - Standing over toys, food bowls, or even a favorite spot to prevent others from taking them.
- Lunging or Biting
    - In severe cases, pets may attack anyone trying to take their resource.

Causes of Resource Guarding

- Instinctual Behavior
    - In the wild, animals protect their food and resources for survival. This instinct persists in domesticated pets.
- Early Life Experiences
    - Pets who experienced food scarcity or competition as puppies or kittens are more prone to guarding.
- Learned Behavior
    - If an animal has had its food or toys taken away frequently, it may develop a defensive response.
- Fear or Anxiety
    - Pets that feel insecure or threatened are more likely to guard their possessions.

Prevention and Management of Resource Guarding

- Early Socialization and Training
    - Expose young pets to different people and experiences around food and toys to build confidence.
    - Handle food bowls, toys, and treats calmly to prevent possessive behavior.
- Desensitization and Counterconditioning
    - Gradually expose the pet to people approaching while eating, rewarding them for calm behavior.
    - Trade valuable objects for high-value treats to teach them that giving up items leads to rewards.
- Avoid Punishment or Forced Removal
    - Taking food or toys away by force reinforces guarding behavior and increases aggression.
    - Instead, use a trade system where they receive something better in exchange.
- Hand-Feeding and Positive Reinforcement
    - Feeding by hand builds trust and reduces the fear of food being taken away.
    - Praise and reward pets when they allow humans near their food or possessions.
- Managing the Environment
    - Feed pets separately if resource guarding is an issue in multi-pet households.
    - Provide multiple toys and food bowls to minimize competition.
- Using Professional Help for Severe Cases
    - If guarding behavior escalates to dangerous aggression, seek guidance from a professional behaviorist or trainer.
    - Medication may be recommended in extreme cases where anxiety plays a significant role.

Addressing Both Behaviors in Multi-Pet Households

Preventing Competition

- Provide individual feeding areas to reduce food guarding.
- Supervise playtime to prevent fights over toys or treats.
- Establish clear boundaries and reward positive interactions.

Teaching Sharing Through Positive Reinforcement

- Reward pets for calm and polite behavior when sharing resources.
- Use structured play and training to build cooperation.
- Gradually introduce shared activities to build trust.

Recognizing Warning Signs Early

- Monitor interactions for signs of stress or aggression.

- Intervene before conflicts escalate.
- Redirect pets to appropriate behaviors using commands and training exercises.

Destructive chewing and resource guarding can be challenging behaviors, but with patience, consistency, and proper training, they can be managed effectively. Understanding the root causes, implementing prevention strategies, and reinforcing positive behaviors will create a balanced and stress-free environment for both pets and owners.

Fear and Anxiety in Dogs: Signs, Causes, and Management

Fear and anxiety are common issues in dogs and can significantly impact their well-being and behavior. Understanding the signs, causes, and management techniques for fear and anxiety is essential for pet owners, trainers, and veterinarians to ensure that dogs live happy and stress-free lives.

Understanding Fear and Anxiety in Dogs

Fear is a natural emotional response to a perceived threat. It is an adaptive survival mechanism that helps animals avoid danger. Anxiety, on the other hand, is a prolonged state of worry or unease, often triggered by uncertainty or past traumatic experiences. While occasional fear is normal, persistent fear or anxiety can lead to serious behavioral and health problems.

Fear and anxiety in dogs can manifest in various ways, including trembling, hiding, aggression, excessive barking, and destructive behaviors. These emotions may be triggered by specific stimuli such as loud noises, unfamiliar environments, or past trauma. In some cases, fear and anxiety may be a result of genetic predisposition, poor socialization, or underlying medical conditions.

Signs of Fear and Anxiety in Dogs

Recognizing the signs of fear and anxiety in dogs is crucial for early intervention. Dogs may exhibit different symptoms depending on the severity of their distress. Common signs include:

- Body Language Changes:
    - Flattened ears
    - Tucked tail
    - Cowering or attempting to make themselves small
    - Dilated pupils
    - Yawning, licking lips, or excessive panting without exertion
    - Trembling or shaking
- Behavioral Changes:
    - Hiding or avoiding interaction
    - Excessive barking or whining

- - Destructive chewing or digging
    - Clingy behavior, constantly seeking reassurance
    - Refusal to eat or loss of appetite
- Aggressive Responses:
    - Growling, snapping, or biting when approached
    - Lunging or barking at perceived threats
    - Defensive postures, such as stiffening of the body or raised hackles
- Physiological Symptoms:
    - Increased heart rate
    - Excessive drooling
    - Involuntary urination or defecation due to stress

Understanding these signs can help pet owners intervene before the fear or anxiety escalates into a serious behavioral issue.

Common Causes of Fear and Anxiety in Dogs

Several factors contribute to fear and anxiety in dogs, and identifying the underlying cause is the first step toward effective management. Some common causes include:

1. Lack of Socialization

Dogs that were not properly socialized during their critical developmental period (typically between 3 and 14 weeks of age) may develop fear and anxiety toward unfamiliar people, environments, and objects. Proper socialization helps puppies learn that new experiences are not threatening.

2. Past Trauma or Abuse

Dogs that have experienced abuse, neglect, or traumatic events—such as abandonment, harsh punishment, or attacks by other animals—may develop long-term anxiety and fear responses. Rescued dogs are especially prone to fear-related behaviors due to their unknown or traumatic pasts.

3. Separation Anxiety

Separation anxiety is a condition in which a dog experiences extreme distress when left alone. It often manifests through destructive behavior, excessive barking, pacing, and attempts to escape. This condition is commonly seen in dogs that have been rehomed multiple times, have a strong attachment to their owners, or have never been taught to be comfortable alone.

4. Loud Noises and Environmental Triggers

Many dogs develop noise phobias, particularly toward thunderstorms, fireworks, vacuum cleaners, or construction sounds. Sudden loud noises can trigger intense fear responses, leading dogs to hide, tremble, or panic. In some cases, they may attempt to escape or injure themselves.

5. Changes in Routine or Environment

Dogs are creatures of habit, and sudden changes—such as moving to a new home, the addition of a new pet or family member, or alterations in daily routines—can cause stress and anxiety. Some dogs struggle with adapting to change, leading to fearful behaviors.

6. Genetic Predisposition

Certain breeds are more prone to anxiety and fear-related behaviors due to their genetic makeup. Breeds such as Border Collies, German Shepherds, and Labrador Retrievers are known for their sensitivity and may be more susceptible to anxiety-related issues.

7. Medical Conditions

Underlying health problems such as pain, neurological disorders, or hormonal imbalances (e.g., hypothyroidism) can contribute to anxiety in dogs. Dogs experiencing chronic discomfort may become more irritable and fearful.

Managing and Treating Fear and Anxiety in Dogs

Effective management of fear and anxiety requires a combination of behavior modification, environmental adjustments, and, in some cases, medical intervention. Here are some proven strategies to help dogs overcome fear and anxiety:

1. Behavioral Training and Desensitization

Desensitization and counterconditioning techniques are commonly used to reduce fear responses. The goal is to gradually expose the dog to the feared stimulus in a controlled manner while rewarding calm behavior.

- Desensitization: Introduce the feared object or situation slowly and in a non-threatening way. For example, if a dog is afraid of the vacuum cleaner, start by placing it in the room without turning it on and rewarding the dog for calm behavior. Gradually increase exposure until the dog is comfortable with it.

- Counterconditioning: Change the dog's emotional response to a feared stimulus by associating it with positive experiences. For example, giving treats and praise when the dog hears fireworks can help reduce fear over time.

2. Creating a Safe and Comfortable Environment

Providing a safe space where the dog can retreat when feeling anxious is essential. This could be a quiet room, a crate with comfortable bedding, or a designated "safe zone" away from loud noises or stressors.

3. Routine and Predictability

Maintaining a consistent routine for feeding, walks, and playtime helps reduce anxiety by giving dogs a sense of stability and security. Dogs thrive on routine and feel safer when they know what to expect.

4. Calming Aids and Supplements

Several natural remedies and supplements can help alleviate anxiety, including:

- Pheromone diffusers (such as Adaptil) that mimic calming mother-dog scents
- Herbal supplements like chamomile, valerian root, and CBD oil
- Calming wraps like the Thundershirt, which provides gentle pressure to reduce stress

5. Exercise and Mental Stimulation

Regular physical activity and mental enrichment help reduce anxiety by providing an outlet for pent-up energy. Activities such as puzzle toys, training exercises, and interactive play can help dogs stay engaged and mentally satisfied.

6. Professional Intervention

For severe cases of fear and anxiety, seeking professional help from a certified dog behaviorist or veterinarian is recommended. In some cases, medication such as anti-anxiety drugs (prescribed by a vet) may be necessary to help manage symptoms while behavioral training is implemented.

Fear and anxiety in dogs can be challenging to manage, but with patience, understanding, and the right approach, most dogs can learn to feel safe and confident in their environment. Identifying the root cause of fear and anxiety is the first step toward effective treatment.

Socialization with People, Dogs, and Other Pets

Socialization is one of the most critical aspects of raising a well-adjusted, confident, and friendly dog. Proper socialization helps dogs feel comfortable in different environments, interact positively with people and other animals, and reduce the likelihood of fear-based aggression or anxiety. Whether you are raising a puppy or working with an adult dog, socialization plays a significant role in shaping their behavior and temperament.

What is Socialization?

Socialization is the process of exposing a dog to a variety of experiences, including different people, animals, sounds, sights, and environments, in a positive and controlled manner. The goal is to help dogs develop confidence and adaptability so they can navigate the world without fear or aggression.

While socialization is most effective when done during puppyhood (between 3 and 14 weeks of age), adult dogs can also benefit from ongoing exposure to new experiences. Proper socialization reduces stress, prevents behavioral problems, and fosters a well-mannered pet.

The Benefits of Socialization

A well-socialized dog is:

- Friendly and confident around new people, animals, and environments.
- Less prone to fear, anxiety, or aggression when encountering unfamiliar situations.
- Comfortable in public settings such as parks, veterinary clinics, and busy streets.
- Easier to train and handle, as they are not overwhelmed by new stimuli.
- More adaptable to changes in routine, home, or lifestyle.

Socializing with People

Introducing your dog to different people in a positive way helps them feel at ease around strangers, children, and visitors.

Steps to Socialize Your Dog with People:

1. Start Early (If Possible)
   Puppies should meet a variety of people—men, women, children, people wearing hats, sunglasses, or uniforms—so they learn that different human appearances and behaviors are normal.
2. Use Positive Reinforcement
   Encourage friendly behavior by rewarding your dog with treats and praise when they greet new people calmly.
3. Expose Your Dog Gradually
   Avoid overwhelming your dog by introducing them to one or two new people at a time in a controlled setting.

4. Allow the Dog to Set the Pace
   Never force your dog to interact. Let them approach new people when they feel comfortable.
5. Encourage Gentle Handling
   Teach children and guests to approach the dog calmly, avoid sudden movements, and respect the dog's space.
6. Take Walks in Different Locations
   Expose your dog to different environments where they can observe and meet people, such as parks, pet-friendly stores, and outdoor cafés.
7. Manage Fear or Shyness
   If your dog is nervous around people, introduce them at a distance and reward calm behavior. Gradually decrease the distance over multiple sessions.

Socializing with Other Dogs

Proper socialization with other dogs helps prevent aggression, fear, and reactivity. Dogs that are comfortable around other canines can enjoy social activities such as playdates, dog parks, and group training classes.

Steps to Socialize Your Dog with Other Dogs:

1. Start with Well-Socialized Dogs
   Begin introductions with calm, well-behaved dogs that have a history of positive interactions with other dogs.
2. Use Neutral Territory
   Introduce dogs in a neutral area (like a park) rather than at home, where territorial instincts may arise.
3. Observe Body Language
   Look for signs of comfort, such as relaxed tails, loose body posture, and play bows. If you notice signs of fear or aggression (stiff body, growling, raised hackles), separate the dogs calmly.
4. Keep Initial Meetings Short
   Start with short, positive interactions and gradually increase the time as the dogs get comfortable.
5. Encourage Play but Monitor Behavior
   Dogs should engage in balanced play, where both parties take turns chasing and pausing. If one dog becomes too dominant or nervous, intervene and redirect attention.
6. Expose Your Dog to Different Sizes and Breeds
   Let your dog meet a variety of dogs to prevent fear of specific breeds, sizes, or play styles.
7. Attend Training or Socialization Classes
   Puppy classes and obedience training sessions provide a structured environment for socialization.
8. Manage Negative Experiences
   If your dog has a negative interaction, redirect their focus and provide positive reinforcement in the next encounter. Never punish fearful behavior, as it can increase anxiety.

Socializing with Other Pets

Dogs that live with or frequently encounter other animals (such as cats, rabbits, or birds) should be introduced carefully to promote harmony and prevent chasing or aggression.

Steps to Socialize Your Dog with Other Pets:

1. Use Controlled Introductions
   Start by keeping your dog on a leash and allowing the other pet to observe from a safe distance.
2. Create Positive Associations
   Reward calm behavior around other pets with treats and praise.
3. Respect Species Differences
   Not all animals enjoy being around dogs. If your other pet is fearful, provide separate spaces to prevent stress.
4. Supervise Interactions
   Never leave dogs alone with small pets (such as rabbits or birds) until you are confident they can coexist peacefully.
5. Teach Impulse Control
   Commands like "leave it" and "stay" help prevent chasing or rough play.
6. Be Patient
   Some animals take longer to adjust than others. Allow them to build trust at their own pace.

Common Socialization Mistakes to Avoid

- Forcing interactions: Never push your dog into situations they find overwhelming.
- Ignoring fear signals: If a dog is scared, move at their comfort level instead of rushing the process.
- Skipping socialization altogether: Lack of exposure can lead to behavioral issues later.
- Allowing negative experiences: One bad encounter can reinforce fear, so always create positive experiences.

Socialization is an ongoing process that helps dogs become confident, adaptable, and friendly. Whether introducing your dog to people, other dogs, or different animals, patience and positive reinforcement are key.

Chapter 6: Advanced Obedience and Specialized Training

Building on basic commands, advanced obedience and specialized training refine a dog's skills, enhancing reliability, focus, and responsiveness. This chapter explores advanced techniques, task-specific training, and strategies for shaping exceptional behavior in working dogs, service animals, and well-disciplined companions.

Training for Longer Stays, Distance Commands, and Hand Signals

Advanced obedience training goes beyond basic commands, focusing on increasing a dog's reliability, control, and responsiveness even when they are far from their handler. Teaching longer stays, distance commands, and hand signals enhances communication, strengthens trust, and ensures a well-disciplined dog in various environments. These skills are particularly useful for working dogs, service animals, and pet owners who want better off-leash control.

Training for Longer Stays

The "stay" command is one of the most crucial obedience skills, promoting impulse control, patience, and discipline. Extending the duration of a stay requires building a dog's focus and trust while reinforcing their ability to remain in place until released.

Key Benefits of Longer Stays

- Enhances impulse control and patience.
- Prevents unwanted behaviors such as rushing through doors or running into traffic.
- Helps dogs stay calm in stimulating environments.
- Essential for public manners and safety.

Steps to Train Longer Stays

- Establish a Solid Foundation: Ensure your dog reliably understands "stay" for short durations before increasing time.
- Use a Clear Release Cue: A consistent cue such as "okay" or "free" signals when they are allowed to move.
- Gradually Increase Time: Start by extending the stay by a few extra seconds, then gradually work up to minutes.
- Reward Intermittently: Use variable reinforcement—sometimes rewarding at different intervals—to keep your dog engaged.

- Add Distractions: Introduce mild distractions (toys, sounds, movement) before progressing to more challenging environments.
- Increase Distance: Gradually step away from your dog while reinforcing their ability to remain in place.
- Practice in Different Settings: Train in various locations, including parks, busy streets, and indoors, to generalize the behavior.

Training for Distance Commands

Teaching a dog to obey commands from a distance builds confidence and independence while ensuring they remain responsive in all situations. Distance training is valuable for off-leash control, emergency situations, and working dog tasks.

Key Benefits of Distance Commands

- Strengthens trust and off-leash reliability.
- Increases safety by allowing handlers to control dogs from afar.
- Helps in real-life scenarios such as recalling a dog away from danger.
- Useful for sports, agility, and service work.

Steps to Train Distance Commands

- Start with Short Distances: Begin by standing a few feet away when giving a command such as "sit" or "down."
- Use a Strong Foundation: Ensure your dog fully understands the commands before adding distance.
- Take Small Steps Backward: Gradually increase the space between you and your dog while giving commands.
- Use Clear Visual and Verbal Cues: Maintain eye contact and use an enthusiastic tone.
- Reward for Compliance: Reinforce success with praise, treats, or toys when your dog responds correctly.
- Introduce Environmental Challenges: Train in locations with distractions to solidify the skill.
- Use a Long Training Leash: A long line helps maintain control while practicing off-leash distances.
- Fade the Leash Over Time: Gradually remove leash dependence once your dog reliably follows commands at a distance.

Training for Hand Signals

Hand signals create a silent form of communication between handlers and dogs, useful in loud environments, competitive obedience, and for hearing-impaired dogs. Many dogs naturally respond well to visual cues, making hand signals an effective alternative or supplement to verbal commands.

Key Benefits of Hand Signals

- Enhances communication and responsiveness.
- Useful for training deaf or hard-of-hearing dogs.
- Strengthens focus by encouraging visual attention to the handler.
- Provides a quiet command system for service and working dogs.

Common Hand Signals and How to Teach Them

- Sit: Raise your hand with your palm facing up. Start by pairing the motion with the verbal cue "sit" and reward compliance.
- Down: Move your hand downward with an open palm. Gradually phase out the verbal cue as your dog learns to respond visually.
- Stay: Hold your palm out in a "stop" motion. Reinforce with treats and gradually increase the duration.
- Come: Extend your arm outward and then bring it toward your chest. Pair with the verbal "come" command initially.
- Heel: Pat your thigh or use a sweeping hand motion to signal your dog to walk beside you.
- Leave It: Hold your palm open and move it slightly away from your dog's focus. Reinforce with rewards when they obey.

Steps to Train Hand Signals

- Use Clear, Consistent Motions: Make each signal distinct and repeatable.
- Pair with Verbal Cues Initially: Introduce the hand signal alongside the spoken command.
- Fade the Verbal Cue Over Time: Gradually rely more on the hand signal until the verbal command is unnecessary.
- Reward Prompt Responses: Reinforce with praise and treats to strengthen understanding.
- Train in Different Environments: Practice in various locations to ensure reliability in all situations.

Combining Skills for Advanced Obedience

For well-rounded training, integrate longer stays, distance commands, and hand signals into real-life scenarios. Practicing these skills together creates a highly disciplined, responsive, and confident dog.

- Long Stay with Distance Recall: Command your dog to "stay" and gradually increase your distance before calling them to "come."

- Silent Commands: Use only hand signals in a quiet setting to test your dog's responsiveness.
- Emergency Distance Control: Train your dog to "sit" or "stay" from afar in situations where they must pause before moving toward you.
- Practice with Distractions: Reinforce skills in busy environments to enhance focus and self-control.

Training for longer stays, distance commands, and hand signals strengthens obedience, safety, and communication. These advanced skills help dogs become well-mannered companions, reliable working partners, and responsive pets in all situations. With patience, consistency, and positive reinforcement, dogs can master these essential techniques for a lifetime of trust and teamwork.

Clicker Training: How It Works and Step-by-Step Guide

Clicker training is one of the most effective, science-backed methods for teaching dogs new behaviors. It uses a small handheld device that produces a distinct clicking sound to mark desired behaviors, making training clear and engaging for dogs. This method relies on positive reinforcement, helping dogs learn quickly while strengthening the bond between pet and owner.

Clicker training is widely used for basic obedience, advanced tricks, behavioral modification, and even service dog training. Understanding how it works and following a structured step-by-step approach will set the foundation for success.

How Clicker Training Works

Clicker training is based on operant conditioning, a concept developed by psychologist B.F. Skinner. The principle involves marking a behavior with a distinct sound (the click) and following it with a reward (typically a treat or praise). This helps dogs associate the behavior with positive outcomes, making them more likely to repeat it.

Why Clicker Training Works So Well

- Clear and Immediate Communication – The sound of the clicker provides instant feedback, eliminating confusion.
- Precision in Training – The click pinpoints the exact moment the dog performs the correct behavior, reinforcing learning.
- Stronger Bond Between Dog and Trainer – The positive reinforcement approach builds trust and engagement.
- Effective for All Dogs – Clicker training works for puppies, adult dogs, rescue dogs, and even those with behavioral challenges.
- Encourages Active Learning – Dogs become eager to offer behaviors to earn rewards, speeding up training progress.

Step-by-Step Guide to Clicker Training

Step 1: Choosing the Right Clicker

Clickers come in various shapes and sounds. Some are louder, while others are softer, making them suitable for noise-sensitive dogs. If needed, a retractable pen, tongue click, or a soft clicker can be used as an alternative. The key is to be consistent with the sound.

Step 2: Charging the Clicker (Creating the Association)

Before using the clicker for training, the dog must learn that the click sound predicts a reward. This is called "charging" the clicker.

- Find a quiet space with minimal distractions.
- Have a handful of small, high-value treats.
- Click the device once and immediately give a treat.
- Repeat this process 10-15 times in a row.
- Watch for signs that your dog is making the connection—such as perking ears, looking expectantly, or wagging their tail at the sound.

Once your dog consistently responds to the click with excitement, the clicker is charged and ready for training.

Step 3: Introducing Clicker Training for Basic Behaviors

After charging the clicker, begin associating it with specific actions. Start with simple behaviors your dog naturally performs, such as sitting, lying down, or making eye contact.

- Wait for the behavior to occur naturally.
- The moment the behavior happens, click immediately and follow with a treat.
- Repeat the process to reinforce the behavior.

For example:

- If your dog sits, click at the exact moment their bottom touches the ground.
- Immediately give a treat to reinforce the action.
- With repetition, your dog will realize that sitting leads to a reward.

Step 4: Adding a Verbal Cue to the Behavior

Once the behavior is happening reliably with the clicker, introduce a verbal command.

- Say the cue just before your dog performs the behavior.
- Click and treat when the behavior happens.
- Repeat multiple times until your dog associates the command with the action.

For example:

- Say "Sit" just before your dog naturally sits.
- Click the moment they sit and reward them.
- Over time, they will begin responding to the verbal cue alone.

Step 5: Shaping More Complex Behaviors

Once your dog understands the basics, use shaping to teach more complex behaviors. Shaping means rewarding small steps toward the final desired behavior.

For example, to teach "Roll Over":

- Click and treat when your dog lies down.
- Click and treat when they shift onto their side.
- Click and treat when they roll onto their back.
- Continue reinforcing small steps until they complete the full roll.

Shaping helps dogs learn multi-step behaviors and tricks efficiently.

Step 6: Using Clicker Training for Problem-Solving

Clicker training is also a great tool for correcting unwanted behaviors. Instead of punishing mistakes, focus on rewarding better alternatives.

For example:

- If your dog jumps on guests, ignore the jumping and click only when they keep all four paws on the ground.
- If your dog barks excessively, click and reward for quiet moments.
- If your dog pulls on the leash, click and reward when they walk beside you.

By rewarding desirable behaviors instead of punishing bad ones, dogs learn what to do rather than what to avoid.

Step 7: Fading Out the Clicker Over Time

Once a behavior is well-established, gradually phase out the clicker and transition to verbal praise and occasional treats.

- Click and reward every time at first.
- As the behavior becomes reliable, click every other time before fading it out completely.
- Eventually, use verbal praise or petting as a reward.

The goal is for the behavior to become second nature so your dog follows commands without expecting a treat each time.

Advanced Applications of Clicker Training

Clicker training isn't just for basic obedience—it can be used in advanced scenarios, including:

- Agility Training – Clicker training helps shape precise movements needed for agility courses.
- Service Dog Training – Used to teach complex service behaviors such as retrieving objects and opening doors.
- Canine Sports – Used in dock diving, rally obedience, and competitive trick training.
- Behavior Modification – Helps anxious, fearful, or reactive dogs learn positive coping mechanisms.
- Scent Detection – Used in training working dogs for search-and-rescue, police work, and medical detection.

Common Mistakes and How to Avoid Them

- Clicking at the wrong time – Timing is everything. Click the exact moment the behavior occurs to avoid confusion.
- Using the clicker as a remote control – The clicker is a marker, not a command tool. Do not use it to get your dog's attention.
- Forgetting to follow with a treat – A click must always be paired with a reward, or it loses meaning.
- Clicking too many times – Click only once per correct behavior. Multiple clicks can be confusing.
- Lack of patience – Some behaviors take time. Stay consistent and celebrate small successes.

Clicker training is a fun, effective, and rewarding way to train dogs.

Using Whistle, Vibrations, and Other Alternative Training Methods

Training a dog effectively requires clear communication, consistency, and reinforcement. While traditional methods such as verbal cues, hand signals, and clicker training are widely used, some situations call for alternative approaches. Whistles, vibrations, and other innovative training tools can provide unique benefits, especially for specific training needs, working dogs, deaf or hearing-impaired dogs, and reinforcing commands at long distances.

Why Use Alternative Training Methods?

Different dogs respond to different training methods based on their temperament, physical condition, and training goals. Alternative training tools like whistles and vibration collars can be particularly useful in the following scenarios:

- Training in Noisy Environments – A loud, consistent whistle carries farther than a human voice, making it useful for outdoor or field training.
- Training Deaf or Hearing-Impaired Dogs – Vibrations and light signals serve as excellent communication tools for dogs who cannot hear verbal commands.
- Distance Training – Whistles and vibrations work well for reinforcing recall and obedience from far away.
- Minimizing Overuse of Verbal Commands – Dogs can become desensitized to constant verbal commands, but alternative cues like a whistle or vibration create a fresh stimulus.
- Enhancing Focus and Attention – Some dogs respond better to physical sensations like vibrations or visual cues rather than sound.

By integrating these methods, trainers can create a flexible and adaptable training system tailored to individual dogs' needs.

Using Whistle Training for Dogs

Whistle training is a powerful tool that helps improve communication between a trainer and a dog, particularly at a distance. The distinct and consistent sound of a whistle carries farther than the human voice, making it ideal for recall and fieldwork.

Benefits of Whistle Training

- Consistent Sound – Unlike voice commands, which can vary in tone and volume, a whistle produces a clear and uniform sound every time.
- Works Over Long Distances – Useful for training in open areas such as parks, fields, and hunting grounds.
- Ideal for Multiple Handlers – If more than one person trains the dog, a whistle ensures consistency in commands.
- Prevents Vocal Strain – Trainers do not need to repeatedly shout commands, reducing stress on their voice.

Step-by-Step Guide to Whistle Training

Step 1: Choosing the Right Whistle

- There are different types of dog training whistles, including silent whistles (high-frequency sounds that humans cannot hear) and pea whistles (which produce a rolling tone).
- Choose a whistle that matches your dog's hearing sensitivity and training environment.

Step 2: Associating the Whistle with a Reward

- Start in a quiet environment with high-value treats.
- Blow the whistle and immediately reward your dog with a treat.
- Repeat this process 10-15 times to create a positive association.

Step 3: Teaching Recall with a Whistle

- Begin by calling your dog in a controlled area.
- Use a whistle command (such as three short blasts) to signal recall.
- The moment your dog moves toward you, reward them with a treat and praise.
- Gradually increase the distance before rewarding.

Step 4: Using the Whistle for Other Commands

- Assign different whistle patterns for different commands:
    - One long blast for "Sit"
    - Two short blasts for "Stay"
    - Three short blasts for "Come"
- Pair each whistle cue with a treat and repeat until your dog consistently responds.

Step 5: Reinforcing Whistle Training in Real-Life Situations

- Practice in outdoor environments with mild distractions.
- Gradually introduce higher distractions while reinforcing with rewards.
- Be consistent—never use different patterns for the same command.

Training with Vibration Collars

Vibration collars are excellent alternatives for dogs that are deaf or need a more tactile form of communication. Unlike shock collars, vibration collars use gentle vibrations to signal commands without causing discomfort.

Benefits of Vibration Training

- Ideal for Deaf or Hard-of-Hearing Dogs – Vibrations serve as a clear signal when verbal commands are ineffective.
- Gentle and Humane – Unlike traditional shock collars, vibrations do not cause pain or fear.
- Enhances Off-Leash Control – Provides a way to communicate with dogs at a distance.
- Helps Redirect Unwanted Behaviors – Can be used as a gentle interruption for barking, jumping, or excessive excitement.

Step-by-Step Guide to Vibration Training

Step 1: Selecting the Right Vibration Collar

- Choose a collar with adjustable intensity settings to suit your dog's sensitivity level.
- Ensure the collar fits comfortably but snugly on your dog's neck.

Step 2: Creating a Positive Association with Vibrations

- Start with a very mild vibration while your dog is relaxed.
- The moment the vibration occurs, offer a treat and praise.
- Repeat this process multiple times so your dog sees the vibration as a positive signal.

Step 3: Teaching Basic Commands with Vibrations

- Associate a vibration signal with a known command.
    - Example: Vibrate the collar, then give the "Come" command.
    - When the dog responds, reward them immediately.
- With repetition, your dog will associate the vibration with the expected action.

Step 4: Reinforcing Good Behavior with Vibrations

- Use vibrations to signal attention and recall.
- If your dog engages in unwanted behavior, a short vibration can serve as a distraction cue.
- Over time, use fewer vibrations as your dog learns to respond to visual or hand signals.

Other Alternative Training Methods

Light and Flash Signals

For deaf or hearing-impaired dogs, visual signals can be highly effective. Flashlights or LED collars can be used in the following ways:

- A flashing light can signal "Come."
- A steady light can indicate "Stay."
- Paired with treats, dogs quickly learn to respond to light cues.

Hand Signals

Hand signals work well for dogs that struggle with verbal commands. Common hand signals include:

- Palm facing up – "Sit"
- Finger pointing down – "Lie Down"
- Open hand moving away – "Stay"
- Wave toward self – "Come"

Scent-Based Training for Visually Impaired Dogs

Dogs with limited vision can be trained using scent cues. Different essential oils or scented markers can be used to:

- Guide a dog toward a desired area.
- Differentiate between rooms or training zones.
- Reinforce commands with a distinct scent for each behavior.

Alternative training methods like whistles, vibrations, light signals, and scent-based cues provide invaluable tools for working with dogs in diverse situations. Whether training a hearing-impaired dog, reinforcing commands at a distance, or simply enhancing focus, these methods offer innovative solutions to improve communication.

Teaching Fun Tricks: Roll Over, Shake Hands, Play Dead, and More

Training your dog to perform fun tricks is not only an entertaining experience but also an excellent way to enhance their obedience, strengthen your bond, and provide mental stimulation. While tricks such as "Sit" and "Stay" are essential for obedience, teaching tricks like "Roll Over," "Shake Hands," and "Play Dead" introduces an enjoyable aspect to training that keeps dogs engaged and eager to learn.

Benefits of Teaching Fun Tricks

Before diving into the step-by-step guides, it is essential to understand the many benefits of trick training:

- Strengthens Bonding – Training builds trust and enhances communication between you and your dog.
- Provides Mental Stimulation – Learning new tricks prevents boredom and can help reduce destructive behavior.
- Improves Obedience – Many tricks reinforce fundamental obedience skills such as focus, patience, and impulse control.
- Increases Confidence – Dogs that learn new tricks gain confidence in their abilities, reducing anxiety and fearfulness.

- Offers Physical Exercise – Tricks like "Roll Over" and "Spin" involve movement, promoting physical fitness.
- Creates Social Enjoyment – Impressing guests with a well-trained dog can be fun and rewarding for both you and your pet.

Step-by-Step Guide to Teaching Fun Tricks

Teaching "Shake Hands" (Paw Shake)

"Shake Hands" is a simple yet impressive trick that many dogs pick up quickly. It teaches polite behavior and is a great way to introduce dogs to paw handling, which can be beneficial for grooming and veterinary care.

How to Teach "Shake Hands"

- Step 1: Have your dog sit in front of you.
- Step 2: Hold a treat in your hand and let your dog sniff it.
- Step 3: Say the cue "Shake" while gently lifting your dog's paw with your hand.
- Step 4: Reward with the treat and praise immediately.
- Step 5: Repeat several times until your dog begins offering their paw voluntarily when they hear the cue.
- Step 6: Gradually reduce the use of treats while continuing to praise your dog for successful shakes.

Teaching "Roll Over"

"Roll Over" is an engaging trick that requires patience and consistency. It's also a great way to get your dog comfortable with handling and movement.

How to Teach "Roll Over"

- Step 1: Start with your dog in a lying down position.
- Step 2: Hold a treat near your dog's nose and slowly move it in a circular motion toward their shoulder.
- Step 3: As your dog follows the treat, they will naturally roll onto their side.
- Step 4: Continue moving the treat so they roll completely onto their back and then onto the other side.
- Step 5: Once your dog completes the full roll, reward them with a treat and praise.
- Step 6: Repeat the process while introducing the verbal cue "Roll Over."
- Step 7: With practice, your dog will learn to associate the cue with the movement.

Teaching "Play Dead" (Bang!)

"Play Dead" is an impressive and dramatic trick where your dog lies motionless on command, often following a hand signal resembling a "gun."

How to Teach "Play Dead"

- Step 1: Start with your dog in a lying down position.
- Step 2: Hold a treat near their nose and slowly move it toward their shoulder.
- Step 3: As your dog shifts to their side, introduce the verbal cue "Bang!" or "Play Dead."
- Step 4: Once your dog is fully on their side and still, reward them with a treat and praise.
- Step 5: Encourage them to stay in position for a few seconds before allowing them to move.
- Step 6: With repetition, your dog will learn to drop into position on cue.

Teaching "Spin"

"Spin" is a fun and energetic trick where your dog turns in a full circle on command.

How to Teach "Spin"

- Step 1: Hold a treat near your dog's nose and slowly move it in a circular motion.
- Step 2: As your dog follows the treat, they will naturally turn in a circle.
- Step 3: Once they complete the spin, reward them with a treat and praise.
- Step 4: Introduce the verbal cue "Spin" as they complete the movement.
- Step 5: Repeat until your dog can spin on cue without needing the treat lure.

Teaching "High Five"

"High Five" is an adorable trick that builds on the "Shake Hands" command but adds a more exciting flair.

How to Teach "High Five"

- Step 1: Start with your dog in a sitting position.
- Step 2: Hold a treat in front of their nose and lift your hand slightly higher than for a paw shake.
- Step 3: Say "High Five" and encourage your dog to lift their paw higher.
- Step 4: As soon as their paw makes contact with your hand, reward them with a treat and praise.
- Step 5: Repeat until your dog consistently responds to the cue.

Teaching "Fetch"

"Fetch" is both a fun and practical trick that provides physical exercise and mental stimulation.

How to Teach "Fetch"

- Step 1: Choose a toy or ball that your dog enjoys.

- Step 2: Encourage your dog to grab the toy and hold it in their mouth.
- Step 3: Toss the toy a short distance and say "Fetch."
- Step 4: When your dog picks up the toy, encourage them to return to you.
- Step 5: Reward with praise and treats when they bring it back.
- Step 6: Gradually increase the distance and encourage consistency.

Tips for Successful Trick Training

- Use Positive Reinforcement – Always reward your dog with treats, praise, or toys for correct responses.
- Keep Training Sessions Short – Aim for 5-10 minutes per session to prevent boredom or frustration.
- Be Patient and Consistent – Some tricks take longer to learn than others. Stay patient and keep reinforcing the behavior.
- Use Clear Cues – Choose simple, distinct verbal commands and hand signals.
- Train in a Quiet Environment First – Reduce distractions when teaching new tricks to enhance focus.
- End on a Positive Note – Finish each session with a trick your dog has mastered to build confidence.

Teaching your dog fun tricks is a fantastic way to engage their mind, improve obedience, and create a stronger bond between you and your pet. With patience, positive reinforcement, and regular practice, your dog will master these entertaining tricks and enjoy the learning process. Whether you are showing off their skills at social gatherings or simply having fun at home, trick training adds joy and enrichment to your dog's life.

Scent Work, Fetch, and Agility Training

Training your dog in scent work, fetch, and agility is an excellent way to enhance their physical and mental abilities. These activities are not only fun but also serve essential roles in developing obedience, discipline, and problem-solving skills. Whether you want to engage your dog in professional sports, keep them active, or simply enjoy interactive playtime, incorporating these training methods into their routine can be highly beneficial.

Scent Work Training

Scent work, also known as nose work, taps into a dog's natural ability to detect and differentiate scents. Dogs have an extraordinary sense of smell, and scent training engages their cognitive skills while providing an enriching experience.

Benefits of Scent Work Training

- Mental Stimulation – Engages your dog's brain and prevents boredom.
- Improved Focus and Obedience – Strengthens their ability to follow commands and concentrate.
- Stress and Anxiety Reduction – A great outlet for nervous or high-energy dogs.
- Enhanced Bonding – Strengthens trust and cooperation between dog and owner.

Getting Started with Scent Work
Basic Scent Training for Beginners

- Choose a Distinct Scent – Use a specific treat, toy, or essential oil (like birch or anise) for training.
- Introduce the Scent – Allow your dog to sniff the chosen scent while rewarding them for interest.
- Hide the Scented Item – Start with easy-to-find locations and gradually increase the difficulty.
- Encourage Searching – Use cues like "Find it!" while guiding your dog towards the hidden scent.
- Reward Success – Praise and treat your dog when they locate the scent.

Advanced Scent Work

Once your dog masters basic scent training, you can increase the challenge:

- Multiple Scent Identification – Train your dog to recognize different scents.
- Indoor and Outdoor Searches – Introduce scent searches in new environments.
- Competitive Nose Work – Consider enrolling your dog in professional scent work competitions.

Fetch is one of the most common and enjoyable games for dogs. It provides great physical exercise while reinforcing obedience and recall commands.

Benefits of Fetch Training

- Provides Physical Exercise – Helps maintain a healthy weight and muscle tone.
- Enhances Obedience – Teaches patience, impulse control, and recall.
- Encourages Playful Bonding – Strengthens your relationship with your dog.

Step-by-Step Guide to Teaching Fetch
Step 1: Choosing the Right Toy

- Use a ball, frisbee, or a soft toy that is easy for your dog to carry.

Step 2: Encouraging Interest in the Toy

- Let your dog sniff and interact with the toy to build excitement.

Step 3: Introducing the Chase

- Toss the toy a short distance and encourage your dog to go after it using an excited voice.
- Reward your dog when they show interest in the thrown toy.

Step 4: Teaching the Retrieval

- When your dog picks up the toy, encourage them to bring it back.
- If they hesitate, try running in the opposite direction to entice them to follow.

Step 5: Reinforcing the Return

- Use the cue "Come" or "Bring it" to teach your dog to return the toy.
- Reward them for bringing the toy closer to you.

Step 6: Teaching Drop It

- When your dog returns with the toy, use the cue "Drop it" and exchange it for a treat.
- Repeat until they drop the toy on command.

Step 7: Extending the Distance

- Gradually increase the distance you throw the toy.
- Reinforce the command with praise and treats for successful fetches.

Agility Training

Agility training is a high-energy activity that involves guiding your dog through obstacle courses, including tunnels, jumps, weave poles, and ramps. It improves coordination, obedience, and overall fitness.

Benefits of Agility Training

- Enhances Physical Fitness – Builds strength, endurance, and flexibility.
- Boosts Mental Stimulation – Encourages problem-solving and quick decision-making.
- Improves Confidence – Helps timid dogs gain courage in new environments.
- Strengthens Obedience – Reinforces focus, recall, and responsiveness to commands.

Getting Started with Agility Training

Step 1: Creating a Basic Agility Course

- Use household items such as chairs for weaving, broomsticks for jumps, and tunnels made from large boxes.
- As your dog progresses, consider investing in professional agility equipment.

Step 2: Teaching Jumps

- Start with a low bar and encourage your dog to jump over it using a treat or toy.
- Use verbal cues like "Jump!" and reward them after a successful jump.
- Gradually increase the height as their confidence grows.

Step 3: Introducing Tunnels

- Shorten a tunnel (or use a large open-ended box) and encourage your dog to walk through it.
- Use treats or a favorite toy as motivation.
- Gradually increase tunnel length and add slight bends for a challenge.

Step 4: Training Weave Poles

- Set up poles (or cones) in a straight line, spaced apart for easy navigation.
- Lead your dog through the poles using a treat in hand.
- Gradually remove the lure and encourage independent weaving.

Step 5: Teaching the A-Frame and Ramps

- If using an agility ramp, start with a low incline.
- Walk your dog up and down using positive reinforcement.
- Reward them for reaching the top and completing the descent safely.

Step 6: Running Full Courses

- Once your dog is familiar with each obstacle, combine them into a short course.
- Guide them through the sequence with verbal cues and hand signals.
- Gradually increase speed and difficulty as they become more confident.

Tips for Success in Training

- Use Positive Reinforcement – Reward-based training keeps your dog motivated and eager to learn.
- Keep Training Sessions Short – 5-10 minutes per session prevents fatigue and maintains engagement.
- Be Patient and Consistent – Every dog learns at their own pace; repetition is key.

- Ensure a Safe Environment – Always use non-slip surfaces and avoid overly challenging obstacles.
- Gradually Increase Difficulty – Start with basic commands and progress to more advanced techniques.

Scent work, fetch, and agility training offer exciting ways to keep your dog mentally and physically stimulated while strengthening your bond. These activities cater to different skill levels and energy levels, making them excellent additions to any dog's training routine. Whether you're looking to develop your dog's problem-solving abilities, encourage interactive play, or prepare for professional competitions, these training methods provide countless benefits.

Chapter 7: Training for Therapy and Service Dogs

Training therapy and service dogs requires patience, consistency, and specialized techniques to develop obedience, emotional intelligence, and task-specific skills. This chapter explores essential training methods to prepare dogs for assisting individuals with disabilities, providing comfort, and performing vital support functions in various environments.

The Difference Between Therapy, Service, and Emotional Support Dogs

Dogs have long been companions to humans, providing love, comfort, and assistance in various ways. However, when it comes to specially trained dogs that serve in medical, emotional, and physical support roles, it is essential to understand the differences between therapy dogs, service dogs, and emotional support dogs. While they all contribute significantly to human well-being, their training, purpose, legal status, and rights differ significantly.

Service Dogs

What is a Service Dog?

A service dog is a highly trained canine that assists individuals with disabilities by performing specific tasks that mitigate the person's limitations. These dogs undergo extensive training to perform duties that their handler cannot do independently due to physical, sensory, psychiatric, or neurological disabilities.

Common Types of Service Dogs

- Guide Dogs – Assist individuals who are visually impaired or blind by navigating obstacles and ensuring safe mobility.
- Hearing Dogs – Alert individuals with hearing impairments to important sounds like alarms, doorbells, or a crying baby.
- Mobility Assistance Dogs – Help individuals with limited mobility by retrieving objects, opening doors, and providing stability.
- Diabetic Alert Dogs – Detect dangerous blood sugar level changes through scent and alert their handler before a medical crisis occurs.
- Seizure Alert and Response Dogs – Detect seizures before they happen and provide assistance during and after an episode.
- Autism Support Dogs – Assist individuals with autism by preventing wandering, providing sensory support, and calming anxiety.

- Psychiatric Service Dogs – Aid individuals with conditions like PTSD, anxiety disorders, or depression by performing tasks such as interrupting panic attacks or providing deep pressure therapy.

Training Requirements

Service dogs require rigorous training that lasts between six months and two years. Training focuses on:

- Task-specific training to assist with the handler's disability
- Advanced obedience training to ensure control in all environments
- Public access training to behave appropriately in public places

Legal Protections and Access Rights

Service dogs are legally recognized under the Americans with Disabilities Act (ADA) and have the right to:

- Access public places, including restaurants, stores, airplanes, and housing
- Accompany their handlers at work or in school
- Travel in public transport without restrictions

Businesses and individuals cannot legally ask for proof of a service dog's certification but can inquire about the specific tasks the dog is trained to perform.

Therapy Dogs

What is a Therapy Dog?

Therapy dogs are trained to provide comfort, affection, and emotional support to individuals in hospitals, nursing homes, schools, disaster relief areas, and other facilities. Unlike service dogs, therapy dogs are not trained for specific tasks related to a disability but are instead selected for their gentle temperament and ability to interact positively with people.

Types of Therapy Dogs

- Animal-Assisted Therapy (AAT) Dogs – Work with healthcare professionals to assist in physical or psychological therapy sessions.
- Facility Therapy Dogs – Provide long-term companionship in places like hospitals and nursing homes, often living on-site.
- Crisis Response Dogs – Offer emotional comfort to victims of disasters, violence, or traumatic events.

Training Requirements

Therapy dogs must undergo socialization and temperament training, which includes:

- Basic obedience training (sit, stay, heel, come)
- Comfortability around new people and environments
- Tolerance for handling and petting by strangers
- Exposure to loud noises, medical equipment, and unpredictable settings

Therapy dogs must pass evaluations conducted by organizations such as the Alliance of Therapy Dogs (ATD) or Therapy Dogs International (TDI) before being certified.

Legal Protections and Access Rights

Unlike service dogs, therapy dogs do not have public access rights under the ADA. They:

- Require permission to enter facilities like hospitals or schools
- Are not allowed in no-pet housing or on airplanes under federal law
- Can be refused entry to public spaces where pets are not allowed

Their role is to provide emotional well-being rather than assist with specific disabilities, which is why they do not receive the same legal protections as service dogs.

Emotional Support Dogs

What is an Emotional Support Dog?

An emotional support dog (ESD) is a companion animal that provides comfort and emotional stability to individuals suffering from mental health conditions such as anxiety, depression, PTSD, or panic disorders. Unlike service dogs, emotional support dogs are not required to undergo specialized training.

Who Can Benefit from an Emotional Support Dog?

- Individuals suffering from chronic anxiety, depression, or PTSD
- Those with panic disorders or emotional distress conditions
- People who require the presence of a dog to manage mental health stability

Training Requirements

Emotional support dogs do not require extensive training beyond basic obedience. Their primary role is to offer emotional comfort through their presence rather than perform specific tasks.

Legal Protections and Access Rights

Emotional support dogs are protected under the Fair Housing Act (FHA), allowing them to:

- Live in no-pet housing without additional pet fees
- Be prescribed by a licensed mental health professional through an ESA letter

However, emotional support dogs do not have public access rights like service dogs, meaning they:

- Are not allowed in restaurants, stores, or public spaces where pets are prohibited
- Do not have guaranteed access to flights under the Air Carrier Access Act (ACAA) (many airlines have removed ESA accommodations)

Key Differences Between Service Dogs, Therapy Dogs, and Emotional Support Dogs

Feature	Service Dogs	Therapy Dogs	Emotional Support Dogs
Purpose	Perform specific tasks for individuals with disabilities	Provide emotional comfort to multiple people in facilities	Provide emotional support to one individual
Training Required	Extensive (6 months to 2 years)	Basic obedience and temperament training	No specialized training required
Legal Protection	ADA, FHA, ACAA	No federal protection, only facility permission	FHA (for housing only)
Public Access Rights	Yes (restaurants, public transport, etc.)	No, only in approved facilities	No public access rights
Who Benefits?	Individuals with disabilities (physical, psychiatric, neurological)	Hospital patients, students, therapy groups, trauma victims	Individuals with mental health conditions
Allowed in Housing?	Yes (protected under FHA)	No special rights	Yes (protected under FHA)

Choosing the Right Type of Support Dog

If you are considering getting a support dog, it is important to choose the right type based on your needs:

- If you have a physical or psychiatric disability and require assistance with daily tasks, a service dog is the right choice.
- If you need a dog for emotional well-being without requiring task-specific help, an emotional support dog may be suitable.

- If you want to provide comfort to others in hospitals, schools, or disaster areas, consider training a therapy dog.

Understanding these differences ensures that both the handler and the dog are properly matched to their respective roles and responsibilities.

Service dogs, therapy dogs, and emotional support dogs each play crucial roles in enhancing the well-being of individuals. While they share the ability to provide companionship and support, their training, legal protections, and responsibilities differ significantly.

Essential Skills and Tasks for Therapy and Service Dogs

Therapy and service dogs play vital roles in supporting individuals with disabilities and providing emotional comfort to those in need. While their functions differ, both require extensive training to develop specialized skills that allow them to perform their duties effectively. Service dogs must master complex tasks that assist their handlers with daily activities, while therapy dogs need to exhibit exceptional social skills, emotional intelligence, and calmness in various environments.

This guide will explore the fundamental skills and tasks that both therapy and service dogs must learn, their training process, and the key differences in their roles.

Foundational Training for Both Therapy and Service Dogs

Before diving into specialized skills, all therapy and service dogs must undergo foundational training to ensure they behave appropriately in public and remain calm in different settings.

Basic Obedience Training

- Sit, Stay, and Down – Essential for maintaining control and discipline in various situations.
- Heel and Loose Leash Walking – Ensures the dog walks beside its handler without pulling.
- Come (Recall Training) – Crucial for safety and ensuring the dog responds when called.
- Leave It and Drop It – Helps prevent dogs from picking up harmful objects.
- Focus and Attention Training – Teaches the dog to remain engaged with the handler, ignoring distractions.

Socialization Skills

Both therapy and service dogs must be well-socialized with:

- Different types of people, including children, elderly individuals, and those with disabilities.
- Other animals to ensure they remain calm around household pets or animals in public settings.
- Noisy and unpredictable environments, such as hospitals, airports, and crowded public spaces.

Essential Skills and Tasks for Therapy Dogs

Emotional Support and Comforting Behaviors

Therapy dogs are trained to provide affection and emotional stability to individuals in hospitals, schools, nursing homes, and disaster sites. They must learn to:

- Offer Physical Comfort – Sit or lie beside a person needing emotional support.
- Provide Deep Pressure Therapy – Lie across a person's lap to create a calming effect.
- Respond to Emotional Cues – Approach and offer comfort when someone appears distressed.
- Accept Petting and Handling – Remain calm when being touched or hugged by multiple people.

Calm and Gentle Temperament Training

- Therapy dogs must remain composed in loud or chaotic environments, such as hospitals or classrooms.
- They must not jump, bark, or react aggressively, even when startled or in the presence of unfamiliar stimuli.
- They should be able to sit for long periods without becoming restless.

Facility Etiquette and Public Behavior

Therapy dogs must be comfortable around medical equipment, such as wheelchairs, hospital beds, and walkers. They are also trained to:

- Walk Slowly and Gently – Especially when working with the elderly or individuals with mobility impairments.
- Stay Calm Around Medical Staff – Avoid interfering with nurses and doctors in hospital settings.
- Recognize When to Offer Support – Approach individuals only when directed by their handler.

Interaction with Large Groups

Since therapy dogs often work in group settings, they must:

- Adapt to different people approaching them at once.
- Remain patient when being petted by multiple individuals.
- Move carefully around people to avoid knocking anyone over.

Essential Skills and Tasks for Service Dogs

Task-Specific Training Based on the Handler's Needs

Unlike therapy dogs, service dogs are trained for highly specialized tasks that directly assist individuals with disabilities. These tasks vary depending on the handler's condition.

Guide Dogs for the Visually Impaired

- Navigating Obstacles – Avoiding curbs, stairs, and hazards in the handler's path.
- Stopping at Crosswalks – Recognizing traffic lights and safely guiding the handler.
- Finding Objects – Locating doors, chairs, or specific destinations when commanded.

Hearing Assistance Dogs

- Alerting to Important Sounds – Recognizing doorbells, alarms, or a crying baby.
- Leading to the Source of the Sound – Guiding the handler to a ringing phone or a knocking door.
- Waking Up a Sleeping Handler – Notifying them of fire alarms or emergencies.

Mobility Assistance Dogs

- Retrieving Objects – Picking up dropped items, bringing medication, or fetching a phone.
- Opening and Closing Doors – Using a rope or specialized handle to assist in mobility.
- Providing Stability – Acting as a brace for individuals with balance issues.

Diabetic Alert and Medical Response Dogs

- Detecting Blood Sugar Changes – Using scent to recognize dangerously high or low glucose levels.
- Alerting the Handler – Pawing or nudging to signal a necessary medical response.
- Retrieving Medication – Bringing glucose tablets or an emergency kit when needed.

Seizure Response Dogs

- Recognizing Seizure Onset – Alerting the handler or caregivers before a seizure occurs.
- Lying Beside the Handler During a Seizure – Preventing injury by acting as a buffer.
- Pressing an Emergency Button – Some dogs are trained to activate an alert system.

Psychiatric Service Dogs

- Interrupting Panic Attacks – Nudging, licking, or lying across the handler's body.
- Creating a Barrier in Crowds – Standing between the handler and others for personal space.
- Guiding the Handler to Safety – Leading them away from overwhelming situations.

Public Behavior and Distraction Training

Service dogs must remain focused on their handlers despite external distractions. They are trained to:

- Ignore food, other animals, or people trying to engage with them.
- Remain calm in high-stress environments, such as airports or crowded places.
- Stay alert and responsive to the handler's commands at all times.

Emergency Response Training

- Service dogs learn to recognize emergencies and take appropriate action.
- Some are trained to alert nearby individuals or press an emergency button.
- They may be taught to wake up their handler if they are unconscious.

Key Differences in Skill Sets

Skill/Task	Therapy Dogs	Service Dogs
Provide emotional comfort	Yes	Sometimes (for psychiatric service dogs)
Perform specific disability-related tasks	No	Yes
Public access rights	No	Yes (protected under ADA)
Trained to assist multiple people	Yes	No (trained for one individual)
Required to remain calm in all settings	Yes	Yes
Socialization with the public	Extensive	Limited (trained to focus on their handler)
Emergency response actions	No	Yes (if trained for medical alerts)

Therapy and service dogs play crucial roles in improving the lives of people with physical, mental, and emotional needs. While therapy dogs provide comfort and companionship in institutional settings, service dogs are trained to assist individuals with disabilities by performing specific, life-changing tasks. Both require proper training, socialization, and behavioral discipline to function effectively in their roles.

Public Behavior and Socialization for Assistance Dogs

Assistance dogs play an essential role in supporting individuals with disabilities by performing specialized tasks and providing critical aid in daily activities. Unlike pets or even therapy dogs, assistance dogs undergo extensive training to ensure they behave appropriately in all public settings. They must remain calm, focused, and unbothered by distractions while performing their duties. Proper socialization and public behavior training are crucial for these dogs to ensure they can navigate different environments confidently and provide reliable support to their handlers.

The Importance of Public Behavior Training

Assistance dogs have the legal right to accompany their handlers in public spaces, including restaurants, stores, public transportation, and workplaces. However, this privilege comes with the responsibility of ensuring that the dog is well-behaved, non-disruptive, and able to function effectively in any setting.

Proper public behavior training ensures that an assistance dog can:

- Stay calm and composed in various environments, including crowded and noisy places.
- Ignore distractions such as food, other animals, loud noises, and strangers attempting to engage with them.
- Respond promptly to commands and perform tasks reliably despite environmental changes.
- Demonstrate appropriate leash manners and controlled movement in tight spaces.
- Avoid jumping, barking, or displaying aggression toward people or animals.

Without these skills, an assistance dog may struggle to perform its duties effectively, leading to potential risks for the handler.

Socialization for Assistance Dogs

Socialization is a crucial part of training assistance dogs, ensuring they are comfortable and confident in various situations. Proper socialization helps dogs develop a stable temperament and reduces anxiety or fear when exposed to unfamiliar environments.

Early Socialization with People

An assistance dog must be comfortable around different types of people, including:

- Children and elderly individuals.
- People using medical equipment such as wheelchairs, canes, or crutches.
- Individuals with varying energy levels, from calm to highly active.
- Strangers in public spaces who may attempt to interact with the dog.

Training Methods for Socialization with People:

- Introduce the dog to various individuals in controlled environments, rewarding calm behavior.
- Gradually increase exposure to people in different settings, such as malls, parks, and hospitals.
- Teach the dog to remain neutral when approached by strangers unless given a command to engage.
- Reinforce polite interactions, such as avoiding jumping up or reacting to sudden movements.

Socialization with Other Animals

While assistance dogs need to remain focused on their tasks, they should also be comfortable around other animals without being distracted or showing aggression.

Key Training Aspects:

- Exposure to other well-behaved dogs in controlled environments.
- Teaching the "leave it" command to ignore distractions from other animals.
- Ensuring the dog remains focused on the handler even when other pets are nearby.

Exposure to Various Environments

Assistance dogs must be prepared to navigate diverse settings, including:

- Busy streets – Walking calmly near traffic, sirens, and large crowds.
- Public transportation – Remaining still and quiet on buses, trains, or airplanes.
- Retail stores and restaurants – Ignoring food and staying settled under tables or beside the handler.
- Hospitals and medical offices – Remaining calm around medical equipment and in high-stress environments.

Gradual Exposure Training:

- Start with quiet locations before progressing to busier environments.
- Reward the dog for remaining calm despite distractions.
- Practice controlled leash walking in various locations to ensure consistent behavior.

Key Public Behavior Skills for Assistance Dogs

Leash Manners and Controlled Walking

Assistance dogs must walk politely on a leash without pulling, lunging, or straying from the handler's side. They should be trained to:

- Maintain a steady pace and match the handler's movement.
- Avoid weaving or stopping suddenly unless commanded.
- Walk through doorways, elevators, and escalators calmly and confidently.

Ignoring Distractions

Assistance dogs must learn to ignore common distractions such as:

- Food on the ground or at restaurant tables.
- Other animals, including pets and wildlife.
- Noisy environments, such as construction sites, train stations, or concerts.
- Strangers attempting to pet or interact with them.

Training should include exposure to these distractions with positive reinforcement for staying focused.

Proper Public Etiquette

Assistance dogs should exhibit impeccable manners in public by:

- Lying quietly under tables in restaurants.
- Sitting or standing calmly beside the handler in crowded areas.
- Remaining silent unless trained to alert the handler.
- Avoiding any begging or soliciting attention from others.

Handling Unexpected Situations

An assistance dog must remain composed when faced with sudden or unexpected situations, such as:

- Loud noises like fireworks or sirens.
- Being bumped or stepped on in crowded areas.
- Encountering unfamiliar or overly excited individuals.

Training Methods for Unexpected Situations:

- Gradual desensitization to loud and sudden noises.
- Positive reinforcement for calm behavior when startled.
- Teaching the dog to seek eye contact with the handler instead of reacting to surprises.

Preparing an Assistance Dog for Real-World Scenarios

Public Access Training

Assistance dogs must undergo extensive training to ensure they can handle real-world scenarios appropriately. Public access training includes:

- Practicing in different public spaces with increasing difficulty.
- Teaching the dog to remain settled for extended periods, such as during long flights or hospital visits.
- Exposing the dog to different types of flooring (carpet, tile, slippery surfaces) to ensure confidence in all environments.

Handler-Dog Communication in Public

A strong bond between the handler and the dog is essential for successful public behavior. The dog must:

- Respond to verbal commands and hand signals promptly.
- Understand subtle cues from the handler, such as shifts in body movement.
- Maintain focus on the handler, even in highly stimulating environments.

Legal and Ethical Considerations

Handlers and their assistance dogs must adhere to laws governing public access rights, such as the Americans with Disabilities Act (ADA). Key considerations include:

- The dog must be trained to perform specific tasks related to the handler's disability.
- The dog should not cause disruptions or pose a threat to others.
- Businesses and establishments can only ask whether the dog is required for a disability and what tasks it is trained to perform—no further proof is required.

Common Challenges and Solutions in Public Training

Challenge: Dog Gets Distracted by Strangers

- Solution: Train the dog to ignore petting attempts using the "focus" command. Reward calm behavior when people approach.

Challenge: Reacting to Loud Noises

- Solution: Gradually expose the dog to various sounds using controlled training. Reward calm responses and avoid reinforcing fear-based reactions.

Challenge: Restlessness in Public Spaces

- Solution: Increase duration training by rewarding the dog for staying settled for longer periods. Provide enrichment toys for added comfort.

Challenge: Overexcitement in New Environments

- Solution: Allow the dog to explore new environments at a controlled pace before engaging in structured training.

Public behavior and socialization are essential aspects of training for assistance dogs. These highly trained animals must navigate diverse environments while remaining focused on their handlers, ignoring distractions, and demonstrating impeccable behavior.

Preparing for Therapy and Service Dog Certification

Therapy and service dogs play essential roles in assisting individuals with disabilities, providing emotional support, and enhancing the overall well-being of their handlers. Preparing a dog for certification as a therapy or service animal requires extensive training, socialization, behavioral conditioning, and adherence to strict guidelines. Whether you are training a service dog to help with physical disabilities, psychiatric conditions, or preparing a therapy dog for emotional support in hospitals, schools, or nursing homes, a structured approach is necessary.

Understanding the Difference Between Therapy and Service Dogs

Before beginning the certification process, it is important to understand the distinction between therapy dogs and service dogs, as each serves a unique purpose and follows different certification protocols.

Service Dogs

Service dogs are highly trained animals that assist individuals with disabilities in performing specific tasks that mitigate their condition. These dogs are protected under the Americans with Disabilities Act (ADA) and are allowed access to public places where other animals are not permitted.

Some common types of service dogs include:

- Guide Dogs – Assist visually impaired individuals with navigation.
- Hearing Dogs – Alert deaf or hard-of-hearing individuals to important sounds.
- Mobility Assistance Dogs – Help individuals with physical disabilities by retrieving objects, opening doors, or providing stability.
- Medical Alert Dogs – Detect changes in blood sugar levels, seizures, or other medical conditions.
- Psychiatric Service Dogs – Assist individuals with PTSD, anxiety disorders, or depression by performing tasks like interrupting panic attacks or creating personal space in crowds.

Therapy Dogs

Unlike service dogs, therapy dogs do not assist a specific individual with a disability. Instead, they provide comfort and emotional support to people in hospitals, schools, nursing homes, or disaster areas. Therapy dogs are not covered under the ADA and do not have public access rights, except where permitted.

Common types of therapy dogs include:

- Facility Therapy Dogs – Work in healthcare or educational settings to comfort patients or students.
- Crisis Response Dogs – Support individuals affected by traumatic events.
- Reading Assistance Dogs – Help children improve literacy skills by providing a non-judgmental reading partner.

Understanding these differences is crucial for selecting the right certification path and ensuring proper training for the dog's intended role.

Choosing the Right Dog for Certification

Not every dog is suitable for therapy or service work. Choosing the right candidate involves evaluating temperament, breed characteristics, health, and trainability.

Key Characteristics of a Good Therapy or Service Dog

Regardless of breed, a successful therapy or service dog should possess the following traits:

- Calm Temperament – Must remain composed in a variety of situations.
- High Trainability – Should be eager to learn and respond well to commands.
- Socialization Skills – Comfortable around people, children, and other animals.
- Confidence – Should not be easily startled by loud noises, crowds, or unfamiliar environments.
- Affectionate Nature – Especially important for therapy dogs that provide comfort to strangers.

Best Breeds for Therapy and Service Work

While any breed can potentially become a therapy or service dog, some breeds excel due to their intelligence, temperament, and adaptability.

- Golden Retrievers – Highly intelligent, affectionate, and eager to please.
- Labrador Retrievers – Loyal, trainable, and gentle with people.
- Poodles – Intelligent, hypoallergenic, and excellent problem-solvers.
- German Shepherds – Highly disciplined and protective, making them excellent for mobility assistance and medical alert work.
- Cavalier King Charles Spaniels – Small, affectionate, and great for emotional support therapy work.

While breed plays a role, individual personality is the most important factor in determining suitability.

Training for Therapy and Service Certification

Training a therapy or service dog requires patience, consistency, and professional guidance. Each type of certification follows different training protocols.

Basic Obedience Training

All therapy and service dogs must master fundamental obedience commands such as:

- Sit – The dog should sit calmly on command.
- Stay – Maintain position until released.
- Heel – Walk beside the handler without pulling on the leash.
- Come – Return to the handler when called.
- Leave It – Ignore distractions such as food, people, or other animals.

Advanced Training for Service Dogs

Service dogs must undergo task-specific training based on the handler's needs. This includes:

- Retrieving Items – Picking up dropped objects or fetching items on command.
- Opening Doors and Cabinets – Using special levers or ropes to assist the handler.
- Alerting to Medical Conditions – Recognizing signs of seizures, low blood sugar, or panic attacks.
- Bracing and Mobility Support – Providing physical stability for individuals with mobility impairments.

Socialization and Public Access Training

Service and therapy dogs must remain well-behaved in public places. Exposing the dog to different environments, people, and situations helps them remain calm and focused in real-world scenarios. Training should take place in:

- Shopping malls
- Restaurants
- Public transportation
- Crowded streets
- Healthcare facilities

This ensures the dog can navigate distractions and maintain composure under pressure.

Certification and Legal Considerations

Once training is complete, certification is the next step.

Service Dog Certification

The ADA does not require service dogs to be formally certified, but many handlers choose to obtain voluntary certification to prove their dog's training. Organizations like Assistance Dogs International (ADI) and the International Association of Assistance Dog Partners (IAADP) offer guidelines and assessments.

Therapy Dog Certification

Therapy dogs must pass an evaluation by recognized organizations such as:

- Therapy Dogs International (TDI)
- Alliance of Therapy Dogs (ATD)
- Pet Partners

Testing involves assessing the dog's behavior in public settings, response to strangers, and overall temperament.

Legal Rights and Responsibilities

- Service Dogs – Have public access rights under the ADA and can accompany their handler anywhere.
- Therapy Dogs – Do not have public access rights but are permitted in specific facilities with approval.
- Emotional Support Animals (ESA) – Different from service and therapy dogs, ESAs do not require training but provide comfort to their owner. They do not have public access rights.

Understanding these distinctions is critical for compliance with federal and state laws.

Maintaining Certification and Ongoing Training

Certification is not a one-time event. Handlers must ensure their dog continues to meet behavioral and training standards. Regular refresher training, evaluations, and continued socialization help maintain certification and effectiveness in their role.

Health and Wellness Considerations

A therapy or service dog's physical and mental well-being directly affects their performance. Proper care includes:

- Regular Veterinary Checkups – Monitoring health, vaccinations, and joint conditions.
- Grooming and Hygiene – Keeping the dog clean, especially when interacting with the public.
- Balanced Nutrition – Feeding a diet that supports overall health and longevity.
- Exercise and Mental Stimulation – Ensuring physical fitness and preventing boredom.

Preparing a dog for therapy or service certification is a rewarding but demanding process. Whether training a dog to assist individuals with disabilities or to provide emotional support to those in need, the key lies in proper selection, structured training, and commitment to excellence.

Chapter 8: Correcting Bad Habits and Unwanted Behaviors

Unwanted behaviors can disrupt training and strain the bond between a dog and its owner. Addressing bad habits with patience, consistency, and positive reinforcement ensures long-term success. This chapter explores effective strategies to correct and prevent undesirable canine behaviors.

Jumping on People: Causes and Solutions

Jumping on people is one of the most common behavioral issues in dogs, especially among young, energetic, and untrained ones. While a jumping dog may seem enthusiastic and affectionate, this behavior can be problematic, particularly when dealing with large breeds, children, elderly individuals, or guests who may feel uncomfortable. Understanding why dogs jump and implementing effective training techniques can help correct this behavior and promote polite greetings.

Understanding Why Dogs Jump on People

Dogs do not jump on people out of defiance or bad intent. Jumping is a natural canine behavior driven by several underlying reasons. By identifying the root cause, owners can apply the most appropriate training techniques.

Common Reasons for Jumping on People

1. Excitement and Greeting Behavior
    - Dogs naturally greet each other face-to-face, and when they see their owner or a visitor, they attempt to get closer to the person's face by jumping up.
    - Puppies often jump on their mother to seek attention, and they carry this instinct into interactions with humans.
2. Seeking Attention
    - Some dogs learn that jumping earns them attention—whether it is positive (petting, talking) or negative (being pushed away, scolded).
    - Even negative attention reinforces the behavior because the dog achieves its goal of engagement.
3. Pent-Up Energy and Lack of Exercise
    - High-energy dogs that do not receive enough physical exercise or mental stimulation may express their excitement through jumping.
    - Dogs with insufficient outlets for energy are more likely to develop hyperactive behaviors.
4. Reinforced Habit from Puppyhood
    - Many owners unintentionally encourage jumping by petting or praising a small puppy when it jumps.

- When the puppy grows into a large dog, this once-cute behavior becomes a problem.
5. Lack of Proper Training
    - A dog that has not been taught an alternative greeting behavior (such as sitting) will continue to jump.
    - Consistency in training is essential to reinforcing good habits.
6. Overexcitement Around New People or Situations
    - Some dogs get overly excited when encountering new people, especially if guests encourage playfulness.
    - Sudden changes in the environment or routine can also trigger excitable jumping.
7. Mimicking Other Dogs
    - Dogs learn by observing other dogs. If one dog in the household jumps on people, others may imitate the behavior.
8. Unintentional Encouragement by Guests or Strangers
    - Visitors may find a dog's jumping endearing and respond with affection, reinforcing the behavior.
    - Even pushing the dog away can be interpreted as a form of play, further encouraging jumping.

Risks and Problems Associated with Jumping

While jumping may seem harmless, it can lead to several problems, especially in certain situations.

Potential Dangers of Jumping on People

1. Injury to People
    - Large, strong dogs can knock down children, elderly individuals, or those with mobility issues.
    - Scratches from nails or accidental bites (if the dog is excited) can cause harm.
2. Reinforcement of Overexcitement
    - Dogs that are allowed to jump may struggle with impulse control in other areas, such as leash pulling or greeting other dogs.
3. Potential for Legal Issues
    - In some cases, a dog jumping on a stranger and causing injury could result in liability issues for the owner.
4. Encouragement of Other Bad Behaviors
    - If jumping is tolerated, the dog may develop other attention-seeking behaviors such as barking, pawing, or nipping.

Effective Solutions for Preventing and Correcting Jumping

Correcting jumping behavior requires patience, consistency, and the use of positive reinforcement training methods. Here are step-by-step strategies to stop a dog from jumping on people.

1. Ignore the Jumping Behavior

- When the dog jumps up, completely ignore them—no eye contact, no touching, no talking.
- Turn your back and cross your arms to remove any form of engagement.
- Only give attention when all four paws are on the ground.

Why It Works:

- Dogs seek attention when they jump. If jumping no longer earns attention, they will eventually stop doing it.

2. Teach an Alternative Greeting Behavior (Sit Command)

- Train the dog to sit as the default greeting behavior instead of jumping.
- Reinforce sitting with rewards (treats, praise) whenever they greet someone politely.
- If the dog starts to jump, withhold rewards until they are calm.

Why It Works:

- Teaching a new behavior replaces the undesired one, making it easier for the dog to understand what is expected.

3. Keep Greetings Low-Key to Avoid Overexcitement

- Excitable greetings encourage jumping. When arriving home, stay calm and do not immediately pet the dog.
- Wait a few minutes before engaging, and only greet the dog when they are settled.

Why It Works:

- Reducing excitement levels prevents the dog from reacting impulsively by jumping.

4. Use a Leash for Controlled Greetings

- When expecting guests, keep the dog on a leash to maintain control.
- Have the guest only interact with the dog once they are calm and sitting.

Why It Works:

- The leash provides an immediate way to prevent jumping while reinforcing good manners.

5. Train Guests and Family Members to Be Consistent

- Everyone in the household and frequent visitors must follow the same rule—no petting or talking to a jumping dog.
- Encourage guests to turn away and only interact when the dog is calm.

Why It Works:

- Inconsistency can confuse the dog, making training less effective.

6. Redirect Jumping with a "Place" Command

- Teach the dog to go to a designated spot (such as a mat or dog bed) when someone enters the home.
- Reward them for staying in place.

Why It Works:

- This gives the dog a clear, structured alternative to jumping.

7. Reinforce Calm Behavior with Treats and Praise

- If the dog remains calm and greets someone without jumping, immediately reward them.
- Use treats, gentle praise, or petting as positive reinforcement.

Why It Works:

- Dogs are more likely to repeat behaviors that result in rewards.

8. Manage Energy Levels Through Exercise

- Provide adequate physical and mental stimulation daily through walks, playtime, and puzzle toys.
- A tired dog is less likely to engage in hyperactive behaviors like jumping.

Why It Works:

- Dogs with excess energy often resort to undesirable behaviors, so meeting their exercise needs can prevent jumping.

9. Use a Training Collar or Harness for Extra Control

- A front-clip harness or gentle leader can be useful for managing excitable dogs in public settings.
- These tools provide more control while reinforcing polite behavior.

Why It Works:

- It discourages jumping by limiting movement and redirecting focus.

Jumping on people is a common but manageable behavior. By understanding why dogs jump and applying consistent training techniques, owners can effectively eliminate this habit. The key to success is consistency, patience, and positive reinforcement—rewarding polite greetings while ignoring unwanted jumping.

Digging, Counter-Surfing, and Stealing Food

Dogs have natural instincts and behaviors that sometimes conflict with household rules. Digging, counter-surfing, and stealing food are among the most common issues that dog owners face. While these behaviors can be frustrating, they are not signs of a bad dog—rather, they stem from instinct, boredom, learned habits, or lack of proper training. Understanding why dogs engage in these behaviors is the first step in effectively addressing and correcting them.

Understanding Digging Behavior

Digging is an instinctive behavior that can be traced back to a dog's ancestors. Wild dogs dig to create shelters, hide food, and search for prey. In a domestic setting, digging may serve various purposes, from entertainment to stress relief.

Reasons Dogs Dig

Dogs may dig due to boredom, excess energy, or simply for fun. A lack of mental and physical stimulation can drive dogs to seek out activities, and digging often becomes a self-rewarding behavior.

Some dogs dig to create a cool spot in the ground, especially during hot weather. This behavior is common in thick-coated breeds that are sensitive to heat.

Certain breeds have a strong prey drive and dig instinctively to search for small animals, such as rodents, burrowing insects, or even underground scents.

Anxiety and stress can lead dogs to dig as a coping mechanism. Separation anxiety, changes in routine, or lack of social interaction may contribute to this behavior.

Dogs may dig along fences in an attempt to escape, either due to curiosity, loneliness, or the desire to explore beyond the yard.

Some dogs bury food, bones, or toys as a natural instinct to store resources for later use.

Solutions for Digging

Providing plenty of exercise and mental enrichment reduces the need for dogs to find their own entertainment through digging. Long walks, interactive toys, and playtime can help burn excess energy.

Designating a specific digging area, such as a sandbox, allows dogs to express their natural behavior in a controlled manner. Encouraging them to dig in this area while discouraging digging elsewhere can be effective.

Addressing any underlying anxiety or stress that may be contributing to the behavior is essential. Offering companionship, interactive toys, or calming techniques can help reduce stress-induced digging.

If the digging is due to heat, providing a shaded area and fresh water can minimize the need for dogs to cool themselves by digging.

Ensuring that fences are secure and that the yard is engaging can help prevent escape-driven digging.

Understanding Counter-Surfing Behavior

Counter-surfing occurs when dogs jump onto kitchen counters, tables, or other surfaces in search of food. This behavior is often rewarding for dogs, as they may find scraps, leftovers, or even an entire meal within reach.

Reasons Dogs Counter-Surf

Dogs are natural scavengers, and the smell of food left on counters can be irresistible. If a dog has successfully found food on the counter once, they are likely to try again.

Dogs that are left alone in the kitchen or unsupervised around food may develop a habit of counter-surfing simply because they can.

Dogs with high food motivation or inconsistent feeding schedules may be more likely to seek out additional food sources.

Boredom and lack of stimulation can lead dogs to explore and investigate their environment, leading to counter-surfing as a form of entertainment.

Solutions for Counter-Surfing

Keeping food out of reach and maintaining a clean kitchen prevents dogs from being rewarded for counter-surfing. Storing food in cabinets, using sealed containers, and keeping countertops clear removes temptation.

Teaching the "leave it" command helps prevent dogs from grabbing food that isn't meant for them. Practicing impulse control exercises can reinforce this training.

Using baby gates or closing doors to prevent access to the kitchen can be an effective management strategy.

Redirecting the dog's attention to an appropriate activity, such as a chew toy or puzzle feeder, provides an alternative to counter-surfing.

Reinforcing good behavior by rewarding dogs for staying off counters and responding to commands helps establish clear boundaries.

Understanding Food-Stealing Behavior

Stealing food from tables, plates, or even people's hands is a common behavior in dogs. While it may seem like bad manners, food-stealing is often driven by instinct, past experiences, or lack of training.

Reasons Dogs Steal Food

Dogs are opportunistic eaters, and if food is left unattended, they may seize the opportunity to grab it.

Dogs that have experienced food scarcity or competition in the past may develop food-stealing behaviors out of fear that they won't get enough to eat.

Inconsistent rules about feeding, such as allowing dogs to eat from plates sometimes but not others, can confuse them and encourage food-stealing.

If a dog has successfully stolen food before, they may continue to try, as the reward reinforces the behavior.

Bored or under-stimulated dogs may steal food as an engaging activity, especially if it results in a reaction from their owner.

Solutions for Food-Stealing

Ensuring that food is not left unattended or within the dog's reach eliminates the opportunity for food-stealing.

Consistently enforcing a rule that food is only given in the dog's bowl helps establish clear boundaries.

Teaching the "off" and "leave it" commands reinforces impulse control and helps prevent food-stealing.

Providing regular meals at consistent times reduces the likelihood of hunger-driven food-stealing.

Avoiding reactions that might encourage food-stealing, such as chasing the dog or engaging in a playful struggle, helps prevent reinforcement of the behavior.

Digging, counter-surfing, and food-stealing are natural behaviors for dogs, but they can be managed and corrected through proper training, consistency, and environmental management.

Chasing Cars, Bikes, or Other Animals

Dogs have a natural instinct to chase moving objects, whether it be a car speeding down the street, a cyclist passing by, or a squirrel darting across the yard. While chasing behavior is deeply ingrained in many breeds, it can be dangerous both for the dog and for others. A dog that chases cars risks severe injury or even death. Similarly, chasing bikes, runners, or other animals can lead to accidents, conflicts, or even legal consequences.

Understanding Why Dogs Chase Cars, Bikes, and Animals

Chasing behavior is deeply rooted in a dog's genetics and instincts. Different breeds may be more prone to chasing than others, but the underlying reasons often stem from prey drive, excitement, boredom, or a lack of proper training.

Prey Drive and Instincts

Many dogs have a strong prey drive, meaning they are naturally inclined to chase fast-moving objects. Herding breeds like Border Collies and Australian Shepherds, hunting breeds like Retrievers and Pointers, and terriers bred to hunt small animals often exhibit strong chasing behaviors. For these dogs, movement triggers an automatic response, making them chase without thinking about the potential dangers.

Excitement and Overstimulation

Some dogs chase simply because they are overly excited. The sight of a moving vehicle, a running animal, or a fast-moving cyclist triggers excitement and impulsivity. If a dog lacks impulse control, they may give in to the temptation to chase without listening to commands.

Boredom and Lack of Mental Stimulation

Dogs that do not receive enough mental or physical stimulation often find their own ways to entertain themselves. Chasing can be a self-rewarding behavior, as it provides excitement and an adrenaline rush. If a dog is left alone in a yard or frequently exposed to passing cars, bikes, or animals, they may start chasing as a way to burn off excess energy.

Reinforcement and Past Success

If a dog has successfully chased a car, bike, or animal before, they may be more likely to repeat the behavior. Even if they don't catch the object they're chasing, the thrill of the chase itself can reinforce the behavior.

Territorial or Protective Instincts

Some dogs chase because they see the moving object as an intruder in their space. This is common in guard dog breeds or territorial dogs that feel the need to protect their home, yard, or owner from perceived threats.

Fear or Anxiety

In some cases, dogs chase out of fear rather than excitement. If they are startled by a fast-moving object, their response may be to run after it as a way of confronting or controlling what they perceive as a threat.

Dangers of Chasing Behavior

While chasing might seem like harmless fun, it poses significant risks to both the dog and the people or animals involved.

Risk of Injury or Death

A dog chasing a car can easily run into the road and be hit, leading to serious injury or fatal consequences. Even if the dog avoids the car, sudden stops or falls can result in broken bones, sprains, or other injuries.

Accidents and Legal Consequences

A dog chasing a cyclist or runner may cause them to lose balance and fall, potentially leading to injuries for both the person and the dog. If a dog causes an accident, the owner may be held liable for any damages.

Aggression Toward Other Animals

If a dog chases small animals, such as cats, squirrels, or even livestock, it can lead to aggressive encounters. This behavior can escalate, resulting in injuries or conflicts with other pet owners or wildlife protection laws.

Escape and Getting Lost

Dogs that chase may run far from home in pursuit of their target, increasing the risk of getting lost. If a dog escapes from a leash or yard, they may wander into unfamiliar areas, making it harder for them to find their way back.

How to Prevent and Stop Chasing Behavior

While chasing is a natural behavior, it can be managed and corrected with proper training, consistent boundaries, and environmental management.

Training and Behavioral Modification
Teaching the "Leave It" and "Stay" Commands

Training a reliable "leave it" command helps prevent dogs from engaging in unwanted chasing. Teaching "stay" reinforces impulse control and prevents them from running after moving objects. Consistent practice in controlled environments strengthens their ability to respond even in high-excitement situations.

Impulse Control Exercises

Dogs that chase often lack impulse control. Engaging in training activities such as waiting before meals, sitting before walks, and practicing recall exercises helps reinforce patience and self-control.

Strong Recall Training

A dog with a solid recall (coming when called) is less likely to engage in dangerous chasing behavior. Practicing recall in various environments with increasing distractions ensures that the dog responds even in high-stimulation situations.

Desensitization and Counterconditioning

Gradual exposure to triggers, such as moving bikes, cars, or animals, while reinforcing calm behavior can help reduce chasing tendencies. Rewarding the dog for remaining calm in the presence of moving objects conditions them to respond differently.

Management Strategies

Using a Leash or Long Line

Keeping a dog on a leash or long line during walks or outdoor play prevents them from taking off after a moving object. A secure harness provides better control, reducing the risk of sudden lunges.

Secure Fencing and Yard Management

A sturdy fence prevents dogs from escaping and chasing after cars or animals. Ensuring that fences are high enough and free of gaps helps keep dogs safely contained.

Redirecting Energy to Appropriate Outlets

Providing structured exercise, such as agility training, herding activities, or fetch, satisfies a dog's need to chase in a safe and controlled manner. Engaging their mind with puzzle toys or obedience training reduces excess energy that might otherwise lead to chasing.

Avoiding Triggers When Possible

If a dog has a strong history of chasing, managing their environment to minimize exposure to triggers can be helpful. Walking in low-traffic areas or avoiding places with frequent bike riders or wildlife reduces the likelihood of encounters that could trigger chasing.

What to Do If Your Dog Starts Chasing

Even with the best training and management, a dog may occasionally give in to the urge to chase. Knowing how to respond in these situations can make a difference in preventing accidents.

Stay Calm and Call Your Dog Back

Using a firm but calm voice, call your dog back using their recall command. Avoid yelling, as it may excite or confuse them further.

Use a Distraction

If your dog is mid-chase, creating a distraction, such as making a loud noise, tossing a favorite toy, or using a high-value treat, may break their focus and allow you to regain control.

Never Chase Your Dog

Chasing after a dog that is already in pursuit of something may escalate the situation. Instead, moving in the opposite direction or using a recall command with a positive tone can encourage the dog to return.

Reward Compliance

If the dog returns to you or stops chasing on command, reward them immediately. Reinforcing good behavior encourages them to listen in future situations.

Chasing behavior in dogs is natural, but it can be dangerous if left unmanaged.

Overexcitement, Hyperactivity, and Impulse Control in Dogs

Dogs are naturally energetic and playful, but when excitement becomes excessive or uncontrolled, it can lead to behavioral problems that make daily interactions challenging. Overexcited and hyperactive dogs often have difficulty calming down, focusing, and responding to commands, making them more prone to destructive behavior, jumping, barking, and even aggressive outbursts.

Impulse control is crucial for managing hyperactive behavior and ensuring a well-behaved, balanced dog. Teaching a dog how to regulate their excitement, stay calm in stimulating situations, and respond appropriately to commands enhances their quality of life and strengthens the bond between them and their owner.

Understanding the causes of overexcitement and hyperactivity, along with effective training techniques and management strategies, is essential for creating a well-adjusted, obedient, and relaxed companion.

Understanding Overexcitement and Hyperactivity in Dogs

Overexcitement and hyperactivity are often mistaken for enthusiasm, but they can indicate underlying behavioral issues that need to be addressed.

What is Overexcitement in Dogs?

Overexcitement occurs when a dog becomes excessively stimulated and struggles to calm down. This can happen in various situations, such as when greeting people, during playtime, or when exposed to new environments. Signs of overexcitement include:

- Excessive jumping
- Barking uncontrollably
- Zooming around the house or yard (frantic running)
- Ignoring commands or struggling to focus
- Mouthy behavior or nipping
- Whining or excessive panting

What is Hyperactivity?

Hyperactivity is more than just high energy—it is an inability to settle down, even in low-stimulation environments. Hyperactive dogs often seem restless and engage in constant movement. Signs of hyperactivity include:

- Inability to relax, even after exercise
- Constant pacing, spinning, or fidgeting

- Destructive behavior such as chewing furniture
- Excessive attention-seeking behavior
- Difficulty focusing on training or commands
- Hyperarousal in response to minor stimuli

What is Impulse Control?

Impulse control is a dog's ability to resist immediate urges and respond calmly in various situations. Dogs with poor impulse control struggle with behaviors like:

- Jumping on people instead of waiting for attention
- Darting through doors or pulling on the leash
- Grabbing food or objects without permission
- Overreacting to sounds, movements, or new environments

Causes of Overexcitement and Hyperactivity

Several factors contribute to a dog's tendency to become overexcited or hyperactive. Identifying the root cause helps in addressing the behavior effectively.

Lack of Mental and Physical Stimulation

Dogs need both physical exercise and mental enrichment. Without enough activity, they build up excess energy, leading to hyperactive behavior. High-energy breeds, such as Border Collies, Belgian Malinois, and Labrador Retrievers, require structured exercise and tasks to stay mentally balanced.

Poor Socialization

Dogs that have not been properly socialized may overreact to new people, animals, or environments. They may become overly excited or anxious in situations they are unfamiliar with, leading to frantic behavior.

Reinforced Excitable Behavior

If owners encourage excitable behavior—such as rewarding jumping with attention or engaging in rough play that leads to overstimulation—the dog learns that overexcitement is acceptable and rewarding.

Genetics and Breed Tendencies

Some breeds are naturally more energetic and prone to hyperactivity. Working breeds, sporting dogs, and herding dogs are bred for endurance and high energy, making them more susceptible to excessive excitement.

Poor Training and Boundaries

Dogs that have not been taught impulse control lack the ability to regulate their behavior. Without clear boundaries and consistent rules, they may struggle to calm themselves in stimulating situations.

Anxiety or Stress

Overexcitement can sometimes stem from anxiety. Dogs that feel insecure or uncertain may act out with hyperactive behavior as a coping mechanism.

Diet and Nutrition

A poor diet, excessive carbohydrates, or artificial additives can contribute to hyperactivity in dogs. Feeding a balanced, high-quality diet helps support stable energy levels.

How to Manage Overexcitement, Hyperactivity, and Improve Impulse Control

Exercise and Mental Stimulation
Structured Exercise

Providing adequate physical activity prevents energy buildup that contributes to hyperactivity. High-energy dogs benefit from activities such as:

- Long walks or jogs
- Agility training
- Fetch with structured breaks
- Swimming
- Herding or scent work

Mental Enrichment

Mental stimulation is just as important as physical exercise. Engaging a dog's brain helps reduce hyperactivity. Effective mental exercises include:

- Puzzle toys and treat-dispensing games
- Scent work and nose games
- Basic and advanced obedience training
- Interactive play with commands

Training for Impulse Control

The "Sit and Wait" Command

Teaching a dog to sit and wait before receiving anything they desire—such as food, toys, or going outside—reinforces impulse control.

"Leave It" and "Drop It" Commands

These commands teach a dog to resist the urge to grab objects or lunge toward distractions.

"Calm on Cue" Training

Encouraging a calm state by rewarding relaxed behaviors, such as lying down quietly, helps reinforce self-regulation.

Controlled Greetings and Interaction
Training Calm Greetings

Overexcited dogs often jump on people. Teaching them to sit before receiving attention helps eliminate this behavior. Ignoring jumping and rewarding calm behavior reinforces good manners.

Using Slow Introductions

Introducing new environments, people, or animals gradually prevents overstimulation. Controlled introductions help a dog learn to remain calm.

Creating a Calm Environment
Using Calming Tools

- Soft music or white noise can help dogs relax.
- Calming sprays or diffusers (like Adaptil) can reduce excitement.
- Comfortable resting areas encourage relaxation.

Avoiding Overstimulation

Minimizing excessive excitement helps a dog remain calm. Avoid chaotic play, over-the-top greetings, or activities that promote frantic energy.

Rewarding Calm Behavior

Reinforce calmness by rewarding a dog when they are lying down, waiting patiently, or showing self-control.

Managing Hyperactive Energy with Proper Boundaries

Structured Playtime

Play should have clear boundaries. If a dog becomes overly excited during play, stopping the game until they calm down teaches them to regulate their energy.

Establishing a Routine

Dogs thrive on routine. Consistent feeding, exercise, and training schedules help regulate their energy levels.

What to Avoid When Dealing with Overexcited or Hyperactive Dogs

Reinforcing Hyperactive Behavior

Avoid rewarding excitement with attention. If a dog jumps, whines, or barks excessively, ignoring the behavior instead of engaging with them helps discourage it.

Using Harsh Punishment

Punishing hyperactivity can lead to anxiety and worsen behavioral problems. Positive reinforcement works best to encourage calm behavior.

Inconsistency in Training

Dogs require clear, consistent rules. If one day jumping is ignored and another day it is rewarded with attention, the dog will struggle to understand expectations.

Lack of Down-Time

Dogs need time to rest and decompress. Ensuring they have quiet spaces to relax prevents them from constantly seeking stimulation.

Managing overexcitement, hyperactivity, and impulse control requires patience, consistency, and a balanced approach. Through structured exercise, training, mental stimulation, and clear boundaries, a dog can learn to regulate its energy levels and behave appropriately. By addressing these behaviors early and consistently, owners can enjoy a well-mannered, calm, and happy dog.

Chapter 9: Training for Specific Breeds and Temperaments

Training methods are not one-size-fits-all. Different dog breeds and temperaments require tailored approaches to achieve the best results. Understanding breed instincts, energy levels, and personality traits ensures effective training, fostering obedience, confidence, and a well-balanced relationship between dogs and their owners.

How Training Differs for Different Dog Breeds

Training a dog is not a one-size-fits-all process. Different dog breeds have unique temperaments, energy levels, instincts, and learning capabilities that influence how they respond to training. A method that works well for one breed may not be as effective for another. Understanding breed-specific traits is essential for tailoring training techniques that bring out the best in each dog.

Dogs have been selectively bred for specific purposes over centuries, resulting in a wide variety of working styles, intelligence levels, and problem-solving abilities. While some breeds are highly trainable and eager to please, others are more independent and require specialized techniques. By recognizing these differences, dog owners can ensure successful training outcomes while respecting their dog's natural instincts and personality.

Factors That Influence Training Based on Breed

Instincts and Breed Purpose

A dog's breed determines many of its natural behaviors. Understanding what a breed was originally bred for provides insight into how it thinks and reacts to training.

- Herding breeds (Border Collies, Australian Shepherds, German Shepherds) are highly intelligent and respond well to structured, task-oriented training.
- Hunting breeds (Labrador Retrievers, Beagles, Spaniels) have strong scent-tracking abilities and require training that incorporates their love for retrieving and searching.
- Guarding breeds (Rottweilers, Doberman Pinschers, Mastiffs) are protective and need consistent leadership and socialization to prevent overprotectiveness.
- Companion breeds (Cavalier King Charles Spaniels, Pugs, Bichon Frises) thrive on positive reinforcement and human interaction but may require extra patience.
- Independent breeds (Siberian Huskies, Afghan Hounds, Basenjis) are less motivated by obedience and require creative training techniques.

Energy Levels and Exercise Needs

High-energy breeds require more physical and mental stimulation to stay engaged in training, while low-energy breeds may respond better to shorter sessions.

- High-energy breeds (Belgian Malinois, Border Collies) need training sessions that include interactive games, agility exercises, and mentally stimulating tasks.
- Moderate-energy breeds (Golden Retrievers, Cocker Spaniels) learn well with a balance of structured exercise and obedience training.
- Low-energy breeds (Bulldogs, Basset Hounds) may need motivation through food rewards and patience during training.

Intelligence and Problem-Solving Abilities

Highly intelligent breeds pick up commands quickly but can become bored easily, requiring variety and challenge in training. Less trainable breeds may need more repetition and positive reinforcement.

- Highly intelligent breeds (Poodles, German Shepherds, Dobermans) excel in obedience, trick training, and advanced commands.
- Stubborn or independent breeds (Chow Chows, Akitas, Terriers) require firm, consistent leadership and creative problem-solving methods.

Training Techniques for Different Dog Breeds

Herding Breeds: Border Collies, Australian Shepherds, German Shepherds

Herding breeds are known for their intelligence, strong work ethic, and responsiveness to training. They excel in obedience, agility, and advanced commands.

Training Strategies:

- Use structured training routines to keep their minds engaged.
- Provide mental challenges like puzzle toys and scent work.
- Train with short, high-energy sessions to maintain focus.
- Teach impulse control to prevent nipping or excessive chasing.

Hunting and Retrieving Breeds: Labrador Retrievers, Beagles, Spaniels

These breeds have strong noses and retrieving instincts. They are often food- and toy-motivated, making positive reinforcement effective.

Training Strategies:

- Use scent-based games and retrieving exercises.

- Encourage impulse control to prevent excessive chasing or food scavenging.
- Provide off-leash recall training to reinforce obedience in outdoor settings.
- Utilize reward-based training with food and praise to reinforce good behavior.

Guarding and Protection Breeds: Rottweilers, Doberman Pinschers, Mastiffs

Guarding breeds are naturally protective and require strong leadership and structured training to balance their guarding instincts.

Training Strategies:

- Focus on early socialization to prevent excessive suspicion.
- Establish firm, consistent leadership to maintain control.
- Use controlled exposure to different people and environments.
- Reinforce positive behavior through structured training rather than punishment.

Companion Breeds: Pugs, Cavalier King Charles Spaniels, Bichon Frises

Companion breeds thrive on human interaction and affection. They may be sensitive to harsh corrections and require patience.

Training Strategies:

- Use positive reinforcement and gentle encouragement.
- Keep training sessions short and engaging.
- Socialize early to prevent separation anxiety.
- Focus on house training and basic obedience.

Independent and Stubborn Breeds: Siberian Huskies, Afghan Hounds, Basenjis

Independent breeds are intelligent but less motivated to follow commands. They require patience, consistency, and creative training techniques.

Training Strategies:

- Use high-value rewards to maintain engagement.
- Incorporate fun and interactive activities into training.
- Avoid repetitive drills that lead to boredom.
- Provide physical exercise to prevent destructive behavior.

Toy Breeds: Chihuahuas, Pomeranians, Yorkshire Terriers

Toy breeds may develop "small dog syndrome" if they are not properly trained and socialized. Despite their size, they need firm boundaries.

Training Strategies:

- Use positive reinforcement and rewards.
- Discourage excessive barking through consistent training.
- Train on leash manners to prevent pulling or lunging.
- Set clear expectations to prevent overdependency on owners.

Working Breeds: Dobermans, Boxers, Great Danes

Working breeds are intelligent and task-oriented. They thrive on structure and require purpose-driven training.

Training Strategies:

- Engage them in activities such as agility, tracking, or obedience competitions.
- Provide consistent, firm commands and boundaries.
- Use reward-based training while reinforcing discipline.
- Offer a job or task to prevent boredom and behavioral issues.

Terrier Breeds: Jack Russell Terriers, Bull Terriers, Fox Terriers

Terriers are energetic and independent with strong prey drives. They require firm but fun training methods.

Training Strategies:

- Use short, engaging training sessions.
- Teach impulse control to manage excessive barking and chasing.
- Provide physical and mental challenges to satisfy their energy levels.
- Establish clear rules to prevent stubborn behavior.

General Training Tips for All Breeds

Regardless of breed, there are universal training principles that apply to all dogs:

- Consistency is key – Dogs learn best when commands and expectations remain consistent.
- Patience and positive reinforcement – Reward-based training encourages motivation and strengthens the dog-owner bond.
- Early socialization – Introducing dogs to different people, animals, and environments helps prevent fear-based reactions.

- Regular exercise and mental stimulation – Proper activity levels prevent boredom and destructive behavior.
- Short training sessions – Keeping sessions short and fun prevents frustration and fatigue.
- Clear leadership and boundaries – Establishing leadership builds respect and trust between dog and owner.

Every dog is unique, and training should be adapted to fit their breed characteristics, instincts, and temperament. Understanding how different breeds learn and respond to commands helps create a more effective training experience, ensuring a well-behaved, happy, and balanced companion.

High-Energy vs. Low-Energy Dogs: Adapting Your Methods

Training dogs requires an understanding of their individual energy levels. High-energy and low-energy dogs have vastly different needs, behaviors, and responses to training. While some dogs thrive on rigorous exercise and mental challenges, others prefer a relaxed lifestyle and may be more resistant to high-intensity training sessions. Adapting training techniques to match a dog's energy level is essential for effective communication, engagement, and success.

Dogs were bred for different purposes, which largely influences their energy levels. Working breeds, herding breeds, and sporting breeds typically exhibit high energy, requiring consistent physical and mental stimulation. Conversely, companion breeds, scent hounds, and guardian breeds often have lower energy levels and may need a more relaxed training approach. Understanding these differences ensures that training is both productive and enjoyable for the dog.

Understanding High-Energy Dogs

High-energy dogs are active, intelligent, and often driven by an innate need to work, play, or move. They have a natural enthusiasm for activity and can become easily bored if not provided with sufficient stimulation.

Common Traits of High-Energy Dogs

- Always eager to engage in activity
- Prone to restlessness, jumping, or pacing
- Require extensive daily exercise to remain balanced
- Highly responsive to training but can be easily distracted
- May develop destructive behaviors if understimulated
- Often excel in agility, obedience, and high-energy tasks

Examples of High-Energy Breeds

- Border Collies
- Australian Shepherds
- Belgian Malinois
- Siberian Huskies
- Labrador Retrievers
- Jack Russell Terriers
- German Shepherds
- Dalmatians

Training High-Energy Dogs

Structured Physical Exercise

High-energy dogs require structured exercise before and after training sessions. Physical activities such as running, hiking, fetch, agility courses, and swimming help release excess energy, making them more focused during training.

- Engage in 30-60 minutes of exercise before training to reduce hyperactivity.
- Use interactive games such as frisbee, tug-of-war, and flirt poles.
- Incorporate long walks or jogs to meet their daily exercise needs.
- Provide off-leash play in secure environments to allow for natural energy release.

Mental Stimulation and Advanced Training

Since high-energy dogs are intelligent, they need mental stimulation to prevent boredom and behavioral issues.

- Introduce puzzle toys, scent work, and food-dispensing games.
- Teach complex commands and tricks to keep their minds engaged.
- Rotate training activities to prevent predictability and loss of interest.
- Engage in canine sports like dock diving, flyball, and agility training.

Impulse Control Training

Many high-energy dogs struggle with impulse control, leading to excessive jumping, leash pulling, and difficulty settling down.

- Use "sit" and "stay" commands consistently to reinforce patience.
- Implement structured training sessions that gradually increase self-control.
- Use leash training techniques such as stop-and-go walking and direction changes.
- Reward calm behavior and ignore overexcited reactions to discourage hyperactivity.

Crate and Rest Training

Teaching a high-energy dog to relax and rest is just as important as exercise. Many hyperactive dogs struggle with downtime.

- Train "place" and "settle" commands to encourage calm behavior.
- Provide a comfortable crate or bed as a designated rest area.
- Use calming techniques such as gentle petting and soft music.
- Reinforce rest periods after exercise to promote a balanced energy level.

Understanding Low-Energy Dogs

Low-energy dogs have a more relaxed demeanor and do not require as much physical activity. They are often content with short walks, playtime, and affection. These dogs may take longer to respond to training, but they are usually calm, focused, and willing to learn.

Common Traits of Low-Energy Dogs

- Prefer lounging and napping over intense physical activity
- Tend to gain weight easily due to lower activity levels
- Respond well to calm, patient training techniques
- May take longer to warm up to new commands and activities
- Enjoy bonding with their owners through relaxed interactions
- Often make great therapy or companion dogs

Examples of Low-Energy Breeds

- Bulldogs
- Basset Hounds
- Great Danes
- Shih Tzus
- Pekingese
- Mastiffs
- Newfoundlands
- Bernese Mountain Dogs

Training Low-Energy Dogs

Motivation Through Rewards

Many low-energy dogs are less naturally inclined to participate in training sessions. They often require extra motivation to engage and respond.

- Use high-value treats such as chicken, cheese, or peanut butter to encourage participation.
- Incorporate verbal praise and gentle petting as rewards.
- Keep training sessions short and positive to maintain interest.
- Adjust feeding schedules so that training aligns with mealtimes for increased motivation.

Encouraging Physical Activity

Even though low-energy dogs require less exercise, regular movement is still important for their physical and mental well-being.

- Take multiple short walks rather than long, exhausting ones.
- Use gentle games such as hide-and-seek or light fetch.
- Encourage low-impact activities such as swimming or slow-paced hikes.
- Provide indoor play options like interactive toys or slow-paced tug games.

Patience and Repetition

Low-energy dogs may take longer to learn commands due to their relaxed nature. Training should be slow, steady, and consistent.

- Use a calm, steady tone when giving commands.
- Repeat training sessions frequently, reinforcing commands without frustration.
- Break training into small steps to make learning easier.
- Use gentle leash guidance rather than forceful corrections.

Preventing Weight Gain and Laziness

Low-energy dogs are prone to obesity due to their lower activity levels. Training should incorporate movement to prevent excessive weight gain.

- Use portion control and limit high-calorie treats.
- Encourage playtime and interactive toys to increase daily movement.
- Train during short walks to combine exercise with obedience work.
- Provide food-dispensing puzzles to slow down eating and encourage activity.

Customizing Training for Mixed-Energy Households

Some homes have both high-energy and low-energy dogs, requiring a balanced training approach to accommodate both personalities.

- Separate Exercise Needs – Allow high-energy dogs to burn off excess energy before training sessions while keeping low-energy dogs at a more relaxed pace.

- Modify Play Styles – Use interactive games that both dogs can enjoy, such as controlled tug-of-war or group obedience training.
- Training in Different Environments – Train high-energy dogs in stimulating environments and low-energy dogs in calmer spaces to maximize engagement.
- Manage Feeding and Rewards – Prevent overfeeding lower-energy dogs while using more activity-based rewards for higher-energy breeds.

Understanding a dog's energy level is crucial for developing an effective training strategy. High-energy dogs require structured exercise, mental challenges, and impulse control training to stay focused, while low-energy dogs benefit from patience, motivation, and gentle encouragement.

Training Stubborn, Independent, or Hard-to-Train Breeds

Training a dog can be a rewarding experience, but when dealing with stubborn, independent, or hard-to-train breeds, it requires extra patience, strategy, and understanding. These dogs often have strong-willed personalities, a high level of self-reliance, or a deep-rooted instinct that makes them less eager to follow commands compared to more obedient breeds. However, with the right techniques and a consistent approach, even the most independent dog can learn to follow commands and become a well-mannered companion.

Understanding Stubborn and Independent Breeds

Some dog breeds were developed for jobs that required them to think and act independently. These breeds often exhibit strong problem-solving skills but may resist following direct orders, especially if they see no personal benefit. Understanding the history and instincts of these dogs can help shape training methods that work with their nature rather than against it.

Traits of Stubborn or Independent Dogs

- Strong-willed and determined
- Highly intelligent but not always motivated by pleasing humans
- May ignore commands unless properly incentivized
- Require firm, consistent leadership
- Often get bored with repetitive training sessions
- Can be prone to selective hearing or "testing" boundaries

Examples of Hard-to-Train Breeds

- Afghan Hound (independent and aloof)
- Basenji (strong hunting instinct and self-reliance)
- Siberian Husky (bred for endurance and independent decision-making)

- Shiba Inu (bold and cat-like personality)
- Chow Chow (aloof and strong-willed)
- Bloodhound (highly scent-driven and easily distracted)
- Bulldog (stubborn and slow to respond to commands)
- Dachshund (bred for hunting and digging, making them independent-minded)
- Beagle (strong sense of smell often overrides obedience)
- Scottish Terrier (fearless and determined personality)

These breeds often require a specialized training approach that respects their independence while reinforcing the importance of cooperation.

Key Training Strategies for Stubborn Dogs

Establishing Leadership and Boundaries

Independent dogs respond best to confident, consistent leadership. If they sense weakness or inconsistency, they may take advantage of it and become even more resistant to commands.

- Set clear rules and boundaries from the beginning.
- Maintain consistency in enforcing rules—never allow a behavior one day and punish it the next.
- Use a firm but calm tone when giving commands to establish authority.
- Make sure all family members follow the same training rules to avoid confusion.

Motivation and Reward-Based Training

Unlike naturally obedient breeds that work to please their owners, independent dogs often need a strong incentive to engage in training.

- Use high-value rewards such as cooked chicken, cheese, or favorite toys.
- Find out what motivates your specific dog—some respond better to food, while others prefer playtime or praise.
- Rotate rewards to prevent the dog from getting bored with the same treat.
- Keep training sessions short and engaging to maintain interest.
- Avoid over-relying on treats; mix in verbal praise and interactive play to reinforce positive behavior.

Using a Strong Recall Method

Many independent dogs tend to ignore commands if they are distracted or if they think something else is more interesting.

- Start training recall indoors with minimal distractions before progressing to outdoor settings.

- Use long-line training in open spaces to reinforce recall without the risk of losing control.
- Reward generously when the dog comes when called to make returning to you more appealing than running off.
- Never scold a dog for coming back late—this can create a negative association with recall commands.

Implementing Mental Stimulation

Boredom is often a major cause of stubborn behavior. Independent dogs thrive when given tasks that engage their minds.

- Introduce puzzle toys and problem-solving games to keep them mentally engaged.
- Use scent training and tracking activities for breeds like Bloodhounds and Beagles.
- Rotate toys frequently to prevent boredom.
- Teach advanced tricks or introduce agility training to channel their energy into productive activities.

Leverage Their Natural Instincts

Each breed has instincts that can be used to make training more engaging.

- Hunting breeds (e.g., Beagles, Bloodhounds) respond well to scent-based games.
- Herding breeds (e.g., Border Collies, Australian Shepherds) benefit from structured work, such as obstacle courses.
- Guarding breeds (e.g., Rottweilers, Mastiffs) need clear boundaries and leadership to prevent stubborn defiance.
- Terriers (e.g., Jack Russell Terriers, Scottish Terriers) enjoy digging and searching games that use their problem-solving abilities.

Controlled Socialization and Exposure

Some independent dogs can be aloof, wary of strangers, or reactive in new environments. Proper socialization helps build confidence and reduces training challenges.

- Expose the dog to different environments, sounds, and situations from a young age.
- Arrange positive interactions with different people and other dogs.
- Keep socialization sessions short and positive to prevent overwhelm.
- Use controlled playdates and supervised outings to encourage adaptability.

Overcoming Common Training Challenges

Ignoring Commands

Many stubborn dogs will pretend they didn't hear a command, especially if they aren't motivated.

- Ensure the command has been reinforced with consistent rewards and positive reinforcement.
- Avoid repeating the command multiple times—this teaches the dog they don't have to obey immediately.
- Use leash guidance to reinforce commands during early training stages.
- Increase distance control by training in multiple environments with varying distractions.

Refusing to Walk on a Leash

Some independent breeds resist leash training, either refusing to move or pulling excessively.

- Use a no-pull harness or front-clip leash to prevent resistance.
- Reward the dog for taking steps forward rather than pulling or resisting.
- Avoid dragging or forcing movement—use treats and positive reinforcement instead.
- Gradually introduce new walking environments to build confidence.

Stubborn Potty Training

Some independent dogs take longer to grasp housebreaking rules.

- Set a strict feeding and potty schedule to create a routine.
- Use crate training to encourage bladder control and prevent accidents.
- Take the dog to the same potty spot each time to build familiarity.
- Reward potty success immediately to reinforce the correct behavior.

Dealing with Selective Hearing

If a dog follows commands only when they feel like it, they need to learn that obedience is not optional.

- Use structured training sessions rather than informal commands.
- Implement the "Nothing in Life is Free" method—make them work for food, toys, and attention.
- Reduce distractions during training and gradually introduce new environments.

Training stubborn, independent, or hard-to-train breeds requires patience, consistency, and adaptability. While these dogs may not be as eager to please as others, they are highly intelligent and capable of learning with the right approach. Understanding their natural instincts, establishing clear leadership, and using proper motivation are key factors in ensuring a successful training experience.

How to Work with Rescue and Shelter Dogs

Working with rescue and shelter dogs can be one of the most rewarding yet challenging experiences for dog trainers, adopters, and caretakers. These dogs often come from difficult backgrounds, including neglect, abuse, abandonment, or lack of socialization. As a result, they may exhibit behavioral issues, fear, anxiety, or even aggression. However, with patience, consistency, and the right approach, rescue and shelter dogs can transform into loving, well-adjusted companions.

Understanding the Background of Rescue and Shelter Dogs

Before beginning training or rehabilitation, it is crucial to understand where these dogs come from and what experiences may have shaped their behavior.

Common Backgrounds of Rescue Dogs

- Neglect: Some dogs have experienced prolonged neglect, lacking proper food, shelter, or medical care. They may be underweight, have health issues, or show signs of extreme fear and distrust.
- Abuse: Physically or emotionally abused dogs often display fear-based aggression, submissiveness, or an inability to trust humans.
- Stray Life: Dogs found as strays may have never had proper socialization or training, making them more independent and harder to train.
- Puppy Mill Survivors: Dogs rescued from breeding facilities often suffer from severe fear, lack of socialization, and health issues due to poor living conditions.
- Surrendered Pets: Some dogs are surrendered due to behavioral issues, but many are given up for reasons unrelated to their behavior, such as financial difficulties, allergies, or major life changes in their previous owner's circumstances.

Understanding a dog's background helps in tailoring training approaches to meet their specific needs.

Building Trust and Establishing a Connection

Rescue and shelter dogs may have lost trust in humans, making it essential to establish a strong bond before attempting any form of training.

Creating a Safe Environment

- Provide a calm, quiet space where the dog can feel secure.
- Avoid overwhelming the dog with too much attention or handling in the beginning.
- Use a consistent daily routine to help the dog feel more comfortable.
- Allow the dog to explore their new surroundings at their own pace.

Using Positive Reinforcement to Build Trust

- Offer treats, praise, and gentle petting to encourage positive associations.
- Never force interaction; instead, allow the dog to come to you when they feel ready.
- Use soft and calm tones to communicate.
- Avoid sudden movements or loud noises that may trigger fear.

Understanding Body Language

- A tucked tail, flattened ears, or avoidance may indicate fear or discomfort.
- Lip licking, yawning, or turning away can signal stress.
- Soft eyes, a wagging tail (at a relaxed pace), and leaning into touch are positive signs of comfort and trust.
- Avoid forcing interactions if the dog exhibits fear-based behaviors.

Training Techniques for Rescue and Shelter Dogs

Many rescue dogs have never been trained or may have had negative experiences with previous owners. Training should be focused on patience, consistency, and positive reinforcement.

Basic Obedience Training

- Start with simple commands like "sit," "stay," and "come."
- Keep training sessions short and engaging (5 to 10 minutes at a time).
- Reward small progress to build confidence.
- Be patient—some rescue dogs take longer to learn commands due to past trauma.

House Training and Crate Training

- Establish a feeding and potty schedule to regulate bathroom breaks.
- Use crate training as a safe space rather than a form of punishment.
- Take the dog to the same potty spot every time to create familiarity.
- Reward with praise and treats when the dog eliminates in the correct area.

Leash Training and Socialization

- Some rescue dogs may have never worn a leash, so introduce it slowly and gently.
- Use a harness rather than a collar for dogs prone to pulling or fear responses.
- Start with short walks in a quiet area before gradually introducing new environments.
- Avoid dog parks or busy areas until the dog has built confidence.

Addressing Fear and Anxiety

Many shelter dogs experience fear-based behaviors, which require desensitization and counterconditioning.

- Identify triggers (loud noises, strangers, other animals) and introduce them gradually in a controlled setting.
- Pair exposure to triggers with positive reinforcement (treats, praise).
- Use calming aids such as pheromone diffusers, calming music, or anxiety wraps.
- Never force a fearful dog into an uncomfortable situation; let them progress at their own pace.

Correcting Behavioral Issues

Rescue dogs may have developed unwanted behaviors due to their past experiences. Common behavioral issues include:

- Jumping on people: Teach an alternative greeting, such as sitting for attention.
- Separation anxiety: Start with short departures and gradually increase time away.
- Food aggression: Use hand-feeding techniques and trade-up exercises to create positive food associations.
- Destructive chewing: Provide safe chew toys and redirect destructive behavior.
- Fear of men or specific people: Allow the dog to interact at their own pace with treats and positive experiences.

Helping Rescue Dogs Adjust to a New Home

The First Few Days

- Allow the dog to explore their new home at their own pace.
- Keep interactions calm and low-key to prevent overstimulation.
- Establish a consistent feeding and potty schedule.
- Avoid too many visitors or new experiences in the first few days.

Gradual Introduction to Family Members and Pets

- Introduce new people one at a time in a quiet setting.
- Allow the dog to initiate contact rather than forcing interaction.
- Supervise interactions with other pets and give them time to adjust.
- Use baby gates or leashes to create controlled meetings with resident animals.

Providing Mental and Physical Stimulation

Rescue dogs need both mental and physical activities to help them adjust and prevent anxiety-driven behaviors.

- Use interactive puzzle toys to stimulate their mind.
- Engage in low-stress play sessions such as fetch or tug-of-war.
- Implement short training sessions to reinforce positive behaviors.
- Gradually introduce new environments for exposure and confidence building.

Working with Professional Trainers and Behaviorists

Some rescue dogs have deep-rooted behavioral challenges that may require professional intervention. Seeking guidance from a certified dog trainer or animal behaviorist can be beneficial, especially for:

- Severe aggression toward people or other animals.
- Extreme fear responses that interfere with daily life.
- Resource guarding and food aggression.
- Excessive barking, reactivity, or destructive behavior.

A professional can tailor a behavior modification plan suited to the individual dog's needs, ensuring a smoother transition into a forever home.

Working with rescue and shelter dogs requires compassion, patience, and dedication. Every dog has a unique past that influences their behavior, but with time, understanding, and consistent training, they can learn to trust, bond, and thrive in a new home.

Chapter 10: Training for Special Needs and Senior Dogs

Training special needs and senior dogs requires patience, adaptability, and a compassionate approach. Their unique challenges—such as mobility issues, sensory impairments, or cognitive decline—necessitate tailored methods that focus on comfort, confidence, and maintaining a high quality of life.

Deaf Dog Training: Communicating Without Sound

Training a deaf dog presents unique challenges, but it is entirely possible to teach them to respond to commands, engage in social activities, and thrive in their environment. While sound-based training methods are ineffective, visual cues, hand signals, and body language become the primary means of communication. With patience, consistency, and a positive reinforcement approach, deaf dogs can learn just as well as their hearing counterparts.

Understanding Deafness in Dogs

Causes of Deafness

Deafness in dogs can be congenital (present from birth) or acquired due to age, injury, or illness. Some common causes include:

- Genetic Deafness: Certain breeds, such as Dalmatians, Australian Shepherds, Bull Terriers, and Boxers, have a higher likelihood of congenital deafness, often linked to coat color genetics.
- Age-Related Hearing Loss: Senior dogs may gradually lose their hearing as they age, making it necessary to transition to visual and tactile training methods.
- Infections or Injury: Chronic ear infections, head trauma, or exposure to loud noises can cause partial or complete hearing loss.
- Drug or Toxin Exposure: Some medications or toxins can damage the auditory nerves, leading to permanent deafness.

Recognizing the signs of deafness early can help owners adapt their training methods to better suit their dog's needs.

Signs That a Dog May Be Deaf

Dogs with hearing impairments often exhibit certain behavioral patterns that indicate their loss of hearing:

- Ignoring verbal cues or name calls
- Not reacting to loud noises (doorbells, vacuum cleaners, sirens, or clapping)
- Startling easily when touched or approached from behind

- Barking excessively or in an unusual tone
- Becoming more reliant on visual cues and vibrations

A veterinarian can perform a Brainstem Auditory Evoked Response (BAER) test to confirm whether a dog is completely or partially deaf.

Training Methods for Deaf Dogs

Establishing a Communication System

Deaf dogs rely on visual signals, touch, and vibrations to understand commands and their environment. The key is consistency in the signals used.

- Hand Signals: Use clear, distinct hand signals for each command. American Sign Language (ASL) or custom gestures can be effective.
- Vibrations: Stomping on the floor or tapping on a surface can help grab the dog's attention.
- Touch Training: Light touches on the shoulder or back can be used to signal commands or get the dog's attention.
- Light Signals: Flashing a porch light or using a small flashlight can be an effective recall signal in low-light conditions.

Teaching Basic Commands with Hand Signals

Deaf dogs can learn all the essential commands using hand signals. Here are some commonly used visual cues:

- Sit: A raised palm moving downward.
- Stay: A flat palm held outward (similar to a "stop" signal).
- Come: Arm extended, then brought towards the chest.
- Down: A hand moving downward with a flat palm.
- Good job (positive reinforcement): A thumbs-up or a happy clapping motion.
- No (stop behavior): A wagging index finger or a firm hand signal.

Gaining the Dog's Attention

Since a deaf dog cannot hear verbal calls, alternative ways to gain attention are necessary:

- Light Touch: Gently tap the dog on the back or shoulder.
- Vibrations: Light stomping on the ground can create a sensation the dog feels.
- Wave Motion: A broad wave to catch their eye from a distance.
- Collar Vibrations: Special vibrating collars (not shock collars) can be used to signal the dog in a non-threatening way.

Leash Training for Safety

Because deaf dogs cannot hear potential dangers such as traffic or other animals, leash training is essential.

- Use a harness instead of a collar for better control and comfort.
- Train with a long lead in enclosed areas to practice recall using visual signals.
- Teach directional cues by gently guiding the leash and rewarding correct movements.

Socialization and Play

Deaf dogs can live happy, well-adjusted lives when properly socialized. Since they rely heavily on visual cues and body language, controlled socialization is important.

- Supervised interactions: Introduce new people and pets in a calm environment.
- Teach play signals: Many dogs learn from other dogs, so allowing social play helps them understand visual cues.
- Use engaging toys: Vibrating toys, tug ropes, and scent-based enrichment activities work well.

Preventing Startle Reactions

Since deaf dogs cannot hear approaching people or animals, they may startle easily. Preventing negative reactions requires careful training.

- Approach from the front: Always ensure the dog sees you before making physical contact.
- Wake them gently: If a deaf dog is sleeping, wake them by lightly touching their back or placing a treat in front of their nose.
- Train a positive startle response: Reward calm behavior when unexpected touch occurs to help them build confidence.

Ensuring Safety for Deaf Dogs

Creating a Safe Home Environment

Since deaf dogs cannot hear potential dangers, creating a secure environment is crucial.

- Use fenced yards or leash walking for outdoor time.
- Avoid off-leash play unless in an enclosed, secure area.
- Use a visual recall system such as a flashlight or waving motion.
- Ensure a properly labeled ID tag with "Deaf Dog" clearly indicated.

Special Identification Gear

Using a special collar, harness, or tag that states "I Am Deaf" helps others understand the dog's needs in public settings.

- Brightly colored leashes or vests can help signal their condition to strangers.
- Engraved ID tags or microchips are essential in case the dog gets lost.

Building Confidence and Strengthening the Bond

A deaf dog may initially be more dependent on their owner due to their reliance on visual cues. However, over time, they will gain confidence through training, structure, and positive reinforcement.

- Engage in eye contact games to strengthen non-verbal communication.
- Use high-value rewards such as favorite treats, toys, and praise gestures.
- Develop routines that create consistency and security.

Training a deaf dog requires patience, adaptability, and a commitment to non-verbal communication.

Blind Dog Training: Helping Dogs Navigate the World

Blind dogs can live happy, fulfilling lives with the right training, guidance, and care. While vision loss may present unique challenges, dogs are highly adaptable creatures that rely on their other senses—such as hearing, smell, and touch—to navigate their environment.

Understanding Blindness in Dogs

Causes of Blindness

Dogs may experience blindness for various reasons, either from birth or as they age. Common causes include:

- Congenital Blindness: Some dogs are born blind due to genetic conditions, common in breeds such as Australian Shepherds, Dachshunds, and Collies.
- Progressive Retinal Atrophy (PRA): A genetic disorder that gradually deteriorates the retina, leading to complete blindness.
- Cataracts: A clouding of the eye's lens, common in aging dogs, which can impair vision or cause total blindness.
- Glaucoma: Increased eye pressure that damages the optic nerve, often causing irreversible vision loss.
- Diabetes-Related Blindness: Diabetic dogs are prone to cataracts, which can quickly lead to blindness.
- Trauma or Injury: Physical damage to the eyes or head can result in blindness.

Recognizing the early signs of vision impairment allows owners to take necessary precautions and start training as soon as possible.

Signs That a Dog May Be Blind

A dog experiencing vision loss may display certain behaviors, including:

- Bumping into furniture, walls, or objects
- Difficulty finding food, water, or toys
- Startling easily when approached from the front
- Reluctance to move in unfamiliar environments
- Increased reliance on scent and sound to navigate

A veterinarian can confirm blindness through eye exams and medical tests, helping owners determine the best course of action for training and adaptation.

Training Methods for Blind Dogs

Training a blind dog requires patience, consistency, and a structured approach that emphasizes their remaining senses.

Using Verbal Cues for Communication

Since blind dogs rely heavily on their sense of hearing, verbal commands become essential for training. Clear, consistent voice cues help them understand what is expected.

- Use distinct commands: Keep verbal cues simple and consistent, such as "Step up" for curbs or stairs and "Watch out" for obstacles.
- Provide direction cues: Words like "Left," "Right," and "Straight" help a blind dog navigate new spaces.
- Praise with a happy voice: Since blind dogs cannot see facial expressions, tone of voice is key to reinforcing positive behavior.

Teaching Basic Commands with Sound Associations

Blind dogs can learn standard obedience commands through verbal cues combined with other sensory reinforcements:

- Sit: Use a gentle touch on the back while saying "Sit."
- Stay: Hold a steady hand on the dog's side while saying "Stay."
- Come: Clap or use a whistle to guide the dog toward you.
- Down: Use a touch signal on the chest while saying "Down."

Helping a Blind Dog Navigate Their Environment

Since blind dogs rely on memory and spatial awareness, creating a predictable home layout is crucial.

- Keep furniture in the same place: Frequent rearrangements can confuse a blind dog and cause anxiety.
- Use textured surfaces: Different floor textures (such as rugs or mats) help the dog identify rooms and pathways.
- Provide scent markers: Essential oils or pheromone sprays can mark doorways, stairs, or important areas.
- Establish a consistent routine: Feeding times, walks, and play sessions should be predictable to help a blind dog feel secure.

Training with Sound and Touch Signals

Incorporating sound and touch helps blind dogs feel confident in their environment.

- Tap surfaces: Tapping on the floor with a foot or hand signals direction changes.
- Use a bell: Attaching a small bell to your clothing or another pet's collar allows the blind dog to track movement.
- Guide with touch: A gentle touch on the back or shoulders can direct movement.

Introducing a Blind Dog to New Environments

Slow and Gradual Exploration

When introducing a blind dog to a new space, allow them to explore at their own pace.

- Walk them through the area on a leash first.
- Use verbal encouragement and treats to reward confident movement.
- Let them sniff and investigate objects to build a mental map.

Navigating Outdoor Spaces

Outside environments present additional challenges, such as traffic, unfamiliar surfaces, and unpredictable obstacles.

- Use a harness for better control and guidance.
- Train with verbal direction cues like "Step up" or "Step down" for curbs and stairs.
- Keep walks consistent to build confidence in familiar routes.

Preventing Startle Reactions

Since blind dogs cannot see approaching people or objects, they may startle more easily. Training them to remain calm when surprised is important.

- Announce your presence: Speak before touching the dog so they are not startled.
- Use a consistent greeting cue: A phrase like "Hey buddy, it's me" signals your approach.
- Train positive touch responses: Gently touch their side or back before petting them to reduce startle reflexes.

Ensuring Safety for Blind Dogs

Creating a Safe Home Environment

Since blind dogs cannot see potential dangers, certain modifications help prevent injuries.

- Use baby gates for stairs or high areas.
- Cover sharp furniture edges with padding.
- Keep hazardous items like cleaning supplies and cords out of reach.

Using Identification Gear

Special collars, harnesses, and tags can help others recognize that a dog is blind.

- Use a tag that says "I Am Blind."
- Consider a harness with "Blind Dog" written on it for public outings.

Building Confidence and Strengthening the Bond

Blind dogs thrive on trust and consistency. Strengthening the bond between owner and dog helps build confidence.

- Use a calm, reassuring tone in training.
- Engage in scent-based games, like hiding treats around the house.
- Give extra praise and rewards for brave behaviors.

Training a blind dog requires patience, structure, and adaptation.

Training Senior Dogs: Adjusting Methods for Older Canines

Training is a lifelong process for dogs, and senior dogs benefit greatly from continued learning. While aging brings physical and cognitive changes, older dogs can still master new skills, reinforce previous training, and maintain good behavior. Adapting training methods for senior dogs ensures they stay engaged, active, and confident, while also addressing age-related challenges such as reduced mobility, diminished hearing, or cognitive decline. With patience and the right techniques, senior dogs can continue learning and thriving in their later years.

Understanding the Needs of Senior Dogs

As dogs age, their training needs change. They may require slower-paced learning, adjustments for physical limitations, and more positive reinforcement to keep them motivated. Some key considerations when training senior dogs include:

Physical Changes Affecting Training

- Joint Pain and Arthritis: Older dogs may experience discomfort in their joints, making certain movements like sitting, lying down, or jumping difficult.
- Reduced Energy Levels: Senior dogs may tire more quickly, requiring shorter and less physically demanding training sessions.
- Diminished Hearing and Vision: Some older dogs experience hearing or vision loss, requiring modified training cues.
- Slower Reflexes: Reaction times may slow down, so patience and repetition become essential.

Cognitive Changes Affecting Training

- Canine Cognitive Dysfunction (CCD): This is a condition similar to dementia in humans, affecting memory, learning ability, and behavior.
- Increased Anxiety or Confusion: Some senior dogs become more anxious or easily startled, requiring gentler training techniques.
- Changes in Sleep Patterns: Older dogs may experience disrupted sleep, affecting their attention span during training.

Understanding these changes allows for a compassionate and effective training approach tailored to the needs of senior dogs.

Adapting Training Methods for Senior Dogs

Use Gentle, Low-Impact Training Exercises

Senior dogs benefit from exercises that accommodate their aging bodies while still reinforcing obedience and mental engagement.

- Avoid excessive physical exertion: Focus on mental stimulation rather than physically demanding tricks.
- Use softer surfaces: Training on rugs, grass, or padded floors helps reduce strain on joints.

- Modify commands: Instead of asking for a full sit or down, reward partial movements that don't cause discomfort.

Utilize Positive Reinforcement

Older dogs thrive on encouragement and rewards. Use positive reinforcement techniques such as:

- Verbal praise: A warm, happy tone reassures senior dogs and builds confidence.
- Gentle petting: Physical affection strengthens the bond and reinforces good behavior.
- Soft treats: Older dogs may have dental issues, so use soft, easy-to-chew treats as rewards.
- Toy rewards: If a dog enjoys toys, use them as motivational tools during training.

Shorten Training Sessions

Senior dogs may not have the same stamina as younger ones. Keep training sessions brief but frequent.

- Aim for five to ten-minute sessions.
- Train in quiet, distraction-free environments.
- Break up sessions into multiple small lessons throughout the day.

Incorporate Mental Stimulation

Keeping an older dog's mind sharp is just as important as physical activity. Mental exercises help prevent cognitive decline.

- Teach new tricks: Contrary to the saying, senior dogs can learn new tricks! Try simple commands like "touch" or "spin" (adjusted for mobility).
- Use puzzle toys: Food puzzles and treat-dispensing toys keep dogs engaged and mentally stimulated.
- Engage their sense of smell: Hide treats or use scent-based games to encourage problem-solving.

Addressing Common Training Challenges in Senior Dogs

Mobility Issues and Pain Management

Arthritis and joint pain may make it difficult for senior dogs to sit, lie down, or move as they once did.

- Modify traditional commands: Instead of a full "sit," allow a dog to do a relaxed, partial sit.
- Encourage gentle movement: Instead of jumping, use ramps or steps for elevation changes.
- Provide orthopedic support: Soft bedding, ramps, and joint supplements help reduce discomfort.

Training a Senior Dog with Hearing Loss

Hearing loss is common in aging dogs, but training can still be effective using alternative communication methods.

- Use hand signals: Pair visual cues with commands to help dogs understand expectations.
- Train with vibrations: Gently tapping the floor or using a vibration collar (not a shock collar) can get a dog's attention.
- Avoid startling them: Always approach from the front, and use gentle touches to communicate.

Training a Senior Dog with Vision Loss

Dogs with reduced eyesight rely more on sound, scent, and touch for guidance.

- Keep the environment consistent: Avoid rearranging furniture to prevent confusion.
- Use verbal cues clearly: Speak in a consistent, reassuring tone.
- Teach navigation commands: Words like "step up" or "watch out" help guide them safely.

Dealing with Cognitive Decline

Dogs experiencing cognitive dysfunction may forget commands they once knew or display unusual behaviors.

- Be patient: Re-teach commands as if they are learning them for the first time.
- Use high-value rewards: Strong-smelling treats or favorite toys keep them engaged.
- Maintain a routine: Predictability helps reduce confusion and anxiety.

Continuing Socialization for Senior Dogs

Many owners mistakenly believe that senior dogs no longer need socialization. However, continued exposure to people, pets, and new environments helps keep them confident and engaged.

- Introduce new experiences slowly and gently.
- Allow positive interactions with calm, friendly dogs.
- Take them on short outings to keep them comfortable in different environments.

The Importance of Exercise and Enrichment

While senior dogs may not have the same energy as younger ones, they still need regular exercise and enrichment.

- Daily walks: Adjust walking speed and distance based on mobility.
- Low-impact activities: Swimming and slow-paced hikes are excellent for joint health.
- Interactive toys: Keep their minds engaged with treat puzzles and gentle games.

Strengthening the Bond with an Older Dog

Training is not just about obedience; it is also about reinforcing the bond between a dog and their owner. Senior dogs benefit from extra love, attention, and connection.

- Engage in activities they enjoy: Whether it's short walks, gentle playtime, or simply sitting together, spend quality time with them.
- Be patient with them: Older dogs may take longer to learn, but they still appreciate the effort and attention.
- Offer comfort and reassurance: As they age, senior dogs may become more dependent on their owners for guidance and security.

Training senior dogs requires a compassionate approach that accommodates their physical and cognitive changes.

Working with Dogs with Physical Disabilities

Dogs with physical disabilities, whether from birth defects, injuries, illnesses, or aging, can still live full, happy, and active lives with the right training, support, and care. Their limitations may require adjustments in training methods, mobility assistance, and daily routines, but these dogs are just as eager to learn, bond, and thrive as any other. Working with a dog with a disability requires patience, creativity, and understanding to ensure they feel confident and independent while navigating the world.

Understanding Physical Disabilities in Dogs

Physical disabilities in dogs can take many forms, and each condition requires unique training adaptations and lifestyle modifications. Some common physical challenges include:

Mobility Impairments

- Paralysis or Partial Paralysis: Affects the use of one or more limbs, often requiring wheelchairs or mobility aids.
- Amputation: Dogs with missing limbs learn to compensate, but may require support in maintaining balance and mobility.
- Arthritis and Joint Disease: Common in senior dogs, making movement painful and limiting range of motion.

Congenital Disabilities

- Birth Defects: Some dogs are born with deformities, such as missing limbs or spinal issues, which affect their ability to walk or run.

- Dwarfism or Limb Malformations: Can cause difficulty in movement, requiring adaptations to training and exercise routines.

Neurological Conditions

- Degenerative Myelopathy (DM): A progressive disease affecting the spinal cord, leading to weakness and paralysis in the hind legs.
- Vestibular Disease: Affects balance, making it difficult for dogs to stand or move steadily.

Chronic Pain and Orthopedic Issues

- Hip Dysplasia: A genetic condition where the hip joint does not fit properly, causing pain and reduced mobility.
- Intervertebral Disc Disease (IVDD): Affects the spine, leading to pain, nerve damage, and possible paralysis.

Dogs with physical disabilities require customized approaches to training, movement, and daily care.

Training Dogs with Mobility Challenges

Dogs with mobility impairments can still learn new skills, follow commands, and engage in activities with proper adaptations.

Teaching Basic Commands

- Use verbal and visual cues consistently: Some dogs with mobility issues may struggle with physical movements but can still follow voice commands or hand signals.
- Modify traditional training methods: For example, instead of asking a dog with arthritis to sit, reward them for a partial squat or standing still.
- Use positive reinforcement: Praise, treats, and affection encourage learning while building confidence.

Helping Dogs with Wheelchairs or Mobility Aids

- Introduce the wheelchair gradually: Allow the dog to sniff and explore it before putting it on. Reward them for positive interactions with it.
- Start with short sessions: Dogs need time to adjust to moving with a wheelchair or support harness. Keep training sessions brief and positive.
- Encourage smooth movement: Help the dog practice turning, stopping, and maneuvering obstacles using food lures or gentle guidance.

Assisting Three-Legged Dogs (Tripods)

- Support balance training: Tripod dogs may struggle with stability, so exercises that strengthen their core and remaining limbs help.
- Modify activities: Instead of jumping or climbing stairs, use ramps and lower obstacles.
- Keep an eye on overcompensation: The remaining limbs take on extra weight, so regular vet check-ups help monitor joint strain.

Training Paralysis or Weak-Legged Dogs

- Work on upper body strength: Encourage exercises that engage the front legs, such as pulling toys or weight-shifting activities.
- Use physical therapy techniques: Gentle stretching, hydrotherapy, and massage can improve circulation and flexibility.
- Utilize supportive harnesses: Help dogs move comfortably with slings or rear-support harnesses.

Helping Dogs Navigate Their Environment

Adapting the home and outdoor spaces ensures dogs with physical disabilities can move safely and confidently.

Modifying the Home for Accessibility

- Use ramps instead of stairs: Makes movement easier for dogs with mobility issues.
- Provide non-slip flooring: Hardwood and tile can be slippery; use rugs or mats for better traction.
- Elevate food and water bowls: Helps dogs with joint pain or mobility issues eat comfortably.

Adjusting Outdoor Spaces

- Create clear pathways: Remove obstacles that could trip or block movement.
- Use soft surfaces: Grass, dirt, or padded surfaces are easier on joints than concrete.
- Supervise playtime: Ensure disabled dogs interact safely with other pets.

Enrichment Activities for Physically Disabled Dogs

Keeping a dog mentally stimulated is just as important as physical exercise.

Interactive Toys and Puzzles

- Food puzzles and treat dispensers: Engage a dog's mind while rewarding them.
- Snuffle mats: Allow them to use their nose to search for treats.
- Slow feeder bowls: Encourage mental engagement during mealtime.

Scent Work and Nose Games

Dogs with mobility issues can still enjoy scent-based games, which provide enrichment without physical strain.

- Hide treats or toys: Encourage dogs to search using their nose.
- Scent training exercises: Teach them to identify specific scents.

Water Therapy and Swimming

For dogs who can tolerate water, hydrotherapy provides gentle exercise without joint strain.

- Supervised pool sessions: Support the dog with a life vest.
- Underwater treadmills: Used in physical therapy to improve strength.

Building Confidence in Physically Disabled Dogs

Dogs with disabilities sometimes develop anxiety or frustration when facing physical challenges. Positive reinforcement and support can help boost their confidence.

Encouraging Independence

- Teach problem-solving skills: Guide them through new tasks and reward their efforts.
- Allow them to explore safely: Use leashes, harnesses, or controlled environments for supervised independence.
- Be patient: Some tasks may take longer to learn, but consistency helps.

Reducing Anxiety and Frustration

- Use calming techniques: Gentle massage, aromatherapy, and soothing music help relieve stress.
- Provide a safe space: A comfortable bed or crate gives them a place to rest.
- Stick to a routine: Predictability helps dogs feel secure.

Training Assistance and Therapy Dogs with Disabilities

Dogs with disabilities can still serve as therapy or emotional support animals. Some dogs with physical impairments excel at comforting others, offering companionship, and spreading awareness about special needs pets.

Therapy Training for Disabled Dogs

- Teach calm, friendly behavior: Reward gentle interactions and patient demeanor.
- Expose them to different environments: Help them get comfortable with hospitals, nursing homes, or schools.

- Encourage positive socialization: Let them meet new people and experience positive human interactions.

Advocating for Special Needs Dogs

- Educate others about disabled dogs: Many people underestimate a physically impaired dog's abilities.
- Showcase their skills and resilience: Social media, events, or community programs can help promote awareness.

Dogs with physical disabilities can lead rich, happy lives with the right support, training, and adaptations. Whether a dog has mobility issues, limb differences, or neurological impairments, patience and creative problem-solving allow them to thrive. These dogs may face obstacles, but their resilience, spirit, and unwavering love make them just as incredible as any other.

Chapter 11: Seasonal and Outdoor Training Challenges

Training a dog outdoors comes with unique challenges that change with the seasons. Weather conditions, distractions, and environmental factors can impact a dog's focus and comfort. Understanding how to adapt training methods ensures consistent progress and safety year-round.

Training in Cold Weather and Snow

Training a dog in cold weather and snow presents unique challenges, from icy surfaces to low temperatures that can affect both the dog and the trainer. Despite these difficulties, cold-weather training can be successful and even enjoyable with proper preparation, safety measures, and adaptations to the environment. By understanding how winter conditions impact a dog's behavior, energy levels, and physical comfort, trainers can ensure productive and safe outdoor sessions.

Understanding How Cold Weather Affects Dogs

Dogs react to cold temperatures differently based on their breed, coat type, size, age, and overall health. Some dogs thrive in snowy conditions, while others struggle with discomfort and cold sensitivity.

Breeds Built for Cold Weather

Certain breeds are naturally suited for colder climates due to their thick double coats, body structure, and historical background in cold regions. These breeds typically have high endurance in snow and ice. Examples include:

- Siberian Huskies
- Alaskan Malamutes
- Saint Bernards
- Newfoundland Dogs
- Bernese Mountain Dogs

Breeds Sensitive to Cold

Short-haired, small, and lean-bodied breeds tend to have lower tolerance for cold weather. These dogs require extra protection when training outdoors. Breeds that are particularly sensitive include:

- Chihuahuas
- Greyhounds
- Doberman Pinschers
- Dachshunds

- Boxers

Effects of Cold Weather on Training

- Reduced Focus: Cold temperatures may make dogs more restless or distracted, leading to difficulty in maintaining concentration.
- Slower Responses: Muscle stiffness in colder weather can affect movement speed and response to commands.
- Shortened Training Sessions: Dogs may tire more quickly or become uncomfortable, limiting the length of effective training periods.
- Increased Excitement: Some dogs become overly energized in the snow, making it harder to maintain discipline.

Essential Preparations for Cold-Weather Training

To ensure effective and safe training, preparation is key. Proper gear, warm-up routines, and environmental considerations help both the trainer and dog stay comfortable.

Choosing the Right Gear

- Dog Jackets and Sweaters: Essential for short-haired and small breeds to retain body heat.
- Dog Boots: Protect paws from ice, snow, and salt, which can cause irritation and injury.
- Reflective Gear: Shorter daylight hours mean training may happen in low-light conditions, making reflective vests or collars important for visibility.
- Waterproof Gloves for Trainers: Keeps hands warm while allowing dexterity to handle treats and leashes.

Paw and Nose Protection

- Paw Balm: Prevents cracks and irritation caused by cold surfaces and salt.
- Regular Paw Checks: Remove ice buildup between paw pads after training sessions.
- Nose Balm: Prevents dryness and cracking from cold air.

Warming Up Before Training

Just like humans, dogs benefit from warm-up exercises to prevent stiffness and injuries. Before beginning training:

- Start with a brisk walk or light play session.
- Encourage stretching by having the dog reach for treats.
- Use gentle massage on joints to stimulate circulation.

Effective Training Techniques for Snowy and Icy Conditions

Training in the snow requires modifications to accommodate slippery surfaces, temperature changes, and distractions.

Adjusting Commands for Snow and Ice

- Practice "Slow" or "Easy" Commands: Helps prevent slipping when walking or running on icy ground.
- Use "Wait" and "Stay" More Frequently: Allows better control in unpredictable conditions.
- Introduce "Watch Me": Keeps the dog focused when snow piles, wind, or new scents become distractions.

Reinforcing Basic Obedience in Snowy Environments

- Practice Recall Commands Frequently: Snow can affect visibility, making a strong recall command essential.
- Use High-Value Treats: Cold weather reduces scent detection, so extra-tasty treats keep the dog motivated.
- Increase Verbal Praise: Dogs may be less willing to respond to food rewards if they are cold or uncomfortable.

Modifying Outdoor Activities to Suit Cold Weather

- Shorter Training Sessions: Instead of one long session, break training into shorter, more frequent segments.
- Use Clear Training Areas: Avoid deep snow or icy patches that could lead to injuries.
- Incorporate Movement-Based Drills: Activities like heeling, figure-eights, and directional changes keep the dog active and warm.

Common Challenges and Solutions in Cold-Weather Training

Challenge: Distracted or Overexcited Behavior in Snow

- Solution: Use focus-based exercises, such as sustained eye contact, to keep attention on the handler. Reward calm behavior with treats and praise.

Challenge: Resistance to Going Outside in Cold Weather

- Solution: Introduce outdoor training gradually. Begin with short sessions and increase duration over time. Use positive reinforcement, such as rewarding the dog as soon as they step outside.

Challenge: Freezing or Refusing to Move

- Solution: Ensure the dog is properly dressed for warmth. If the dog still refuses to move, take breaks inside and use upbeat verbal encouragement to motivate them.

Challenge: Ice and Salt Hurting Paws

- Solution: Use dog boots or paw balm before training. Rinse paws after walks to remove salt or ice melt chemicals.

Alternative Indoor Training for Extremely Cold Weather

When outdoor conditions are too harsh, maintaining training consistency indoors is essential.

Indoor Obedience Training

- Practice Sit, Stay, and Recall in a Controlled Environment
- Work on Mat Training: Reinforces a designated "calm spot" for the dog.
- Use Hallways for Heel Training: Mimics outdoor walking exercises.

Mental Stimulation During Winter

- Introduce Puzzle Toys and Scent Work Games: Engages the dog's brain and prevents boredom.
- Train New Tricks or Reinforce Old Commands: Keeps training consistent without exposure to extreme cold.

Cold Weather Safety Tips for Outdoor Training

- Monitor for Signs of Hypothermia or Frostbite:
    - Shivering, weakness, and lethargy may indicate the dog is too cold.
    - Check ears, paws, and tail for discoloration or swelling.
- Keep Water Available: Cold air can cause dehydration, so always bring fresh water.
- Avoid Prolonged Exposure: Limit training sessions in freezing temperatures, especially for small or short-haired dogs.
- Stick to Well-Lit Paths: Avoid deep snow, frozen lakes, or areas with hidden ice patches.

Training in cold weather and snow requires adaptability, patience, and awareness of a dog's comfort and safety. With proper preparation, protective gear, and modified training techniques, outdoor winter sessions can be just as effective as those in warmer months. Whether reinforcing basic obedience, engaging in recall training, or simply taking short, productive walks, maintaining consistency through seasonal changes ensures continued progress.

Keeping Training Fun in Hot and Humid Conditions

Training a dog in hot and humid weather presents unique challenges, as excessive heat can cause discomfort, dehydration, and even serious health issues. However, with proper preparation, modified training methods, and creative approaches, you can ensure that training remains fun, engaging, and safe for both you and your dog. Adapting to seasonal conditions not only helps maintain training consistency but also strengthens the bond between you and your canine companion.

Understanding the Impact of Heat and Humidity on Dogs

Dogs are more sensitive to heat than humans because they have limited sweat glands and rely primarily on panting to cool down. Some breeds and individual dogs are more susceptible to heat-related issues than others, making it crucial to recognize the risks and adjust training accordingly.

Breeds That Struggle in Hot Weather

Certain dog breeds have a harder time coping with high temperatures due to their physical characteristics, such as thick coats or short muzzles. These breeds include:

- Bulldogs (English and French)
- Pugs
- Boxers
- Shih Tzus
- Huskies
- Saint Bernards
- Chow Chows

Signs of Overheating in Dogs

It's essential to recognize early warning signs of heat exhaustion or heatstroke before continuing with training. These signs include:

- Excessive panting and drooling
- Lethargy or reluctance to move
- Bright red or dark-colored gums
- Vomiting or diarrhea
- Staggering or weakness
- Collapse or unresponsiveness

If a dog shows signs of heat exhaustion, immediately stop training, move to a cooler area, offer water, and wet their body with cool (not ice-cold) water. Severe cases require emergency veterinary care.

Essential Preparations for Training in Hot and Humid Weather

Adjusting the Training Schedule

- Train Early in the Morning or Late in the Evening: These times provide cooler temperatures and reduced sun exposure.
- Avoid Peak Heat Hours: Midday training should be avoided, as asphalt and pavement can become dangerously hot.

Choosing the Right Training Location

- Find Shady Spots: Train under trees, in covered patios, or near water sources.
- Use Indoor Alternatives: If outdoor conditions are too harsh, opt for indoor obedience training, mental stimulation games, or short indoor workouts.
- Seek Areas with Grass: Grass stays cooler than concrete or pavement, which can burn paw pads.

Hydration and Cooling Strategies

- Always Provide Fresh Water: Bring a portable water bowl and encourage regular water breaks.
- Use Cooling Mats or Vests: These help regulate body temperature during and after training.
- Incorporate Water Play: Use sprinklers, shallow kiddie pools, or a cooling mist to keep dogs comfortable.
- Soak a Bandana in Cool Water: Wrapping it around your dog's neck provides additional cooling.

Protecting Paws from Hot Surfaces

- Check the Ground Temperature: Place your hand on the pavement for a few seconds; if it's too hot for you, it's too hot for your dog.
- Use Dog Booties: These protect paws from burns and discomfort.
- Stick to Grass or Dirt Paths: Avoid sidewalks and asphalt, which retain heat longer.

Training Techniques for Hot and Humid Weather

Training in warm conditions requires modifications to ensure dogs stay comfortable while still making progress in their obedience, behavior, and skill development.

Shorten Training Sessions

- Instead of long sessions, break training into multiple shorter periods throughout the day.
- Keep each session between five and ten minutes to prevent overheating.
- Watch for signs of fatigue, and stop immediately if the dog appears uncomfortable.

Incorporate More Low-Intensity Exercises

- Avoid excessive running or strenuous activities.
- Focus on obedience commands such as sit, stay, and recall rather than agility drills.
- Practice slow and controlled movements to minimize exhaustion.

Use More Verbal and Food Rewards

- Reduce physical play rewards like tugging or chasing, which generate heat.
- Switch to verbal praise and light petting as positive reinforcement.
- Offer frozen treats like ice cubes, frozen fruits, or chilled peanut butter as rewards.

Adjust Play-Based Training

- Engage in gentler games like hide-and-seek or scent work, which require less physical exertion.
- Try training sessions in a shallow kiddie pool, encouraging dogs to step in and cool off while learning commands.
- Use a sprinkler system to make training more enjoyable in the heat.

Fun Activities That Double as Training in Hot Weather

Keeping training fun and engaging is key to maintaining a dog's enthusiasm, even in hot and humid conditions.

Water-Based Training Games

- Fetch in Water: If safe, let dogs retrieve floating toys in a shallow pool or lake.
- Sprinkler Chase: Teach dogs to follow commands while running through sprinklers.
- Frozen Toy Search: Hide frozen treats or toys in the yard for a fun and cooling scent game.

Indoor Mental Stimulation

- Puzzle Toys: Mental challenges help reinforce training without the physical strain.
- Scent Training: Hide treats around the house to encourage scent tracking skills.
- Obedience Challenges: Work on stay, leave it, and come in a climate-controlled environment.

Shady or Indoor Agility Work

- Set up lightweight obstacles like tunnels, weave poles, or jump bars under a covered area.
- Use indoor space to work on agility movements in a cooler environment.

Overcoming Common Training Challenges in Hot Weather

Challenge: Lack of Focus Due to Heat Discomfort

- Solution: Keep sessions short and engaging, and reward frequently with refreshing treats.

Challenge: Dog Becomes Lethargic or Unwilling to Train

- Solution: Train in cooler environments and adjust the intensity of exercises.

Challenge: Overexcitement When Training with Water

- Solution: Gradually introduce water-based activities, reinforcing calm behavior before resuming training.

Challenge: Dog Refuses to Walk or Move on Hot Pavement

- Solution: Use paw protection, walk in shaded areas, and bring a cooling mat for breaks.

Alternative Training Options for Extremely Hot Days

When outdoor training isn't practical due to extreme temperatures, indoor training keeps dogs engaged while staying cool.

Indoor Enrichment Activities

- Basic Obedience Training in Air-Conditioned Rooms
- Interactive Food Puzzles for mental stimulation
- Low-Impact Physical Training like light stretching and body-awareness exercises

Treadmill Training

- A safe alternative for structured walking when outdoor conditions are unsafe.
- Introduce the treadmill gradually with positive reinforcement.

Car Training in a Climate-Controlled Vehicle

- Practice desensitization to car rides in a cool, air-conditioned car.
- Work on commands like stay, sit, and down in a parked car.

Training in hot and humid conditions requires a balance between productivity and safety.

Training in Crowded or Noisy Environments

Training a dog in a crowded or noisy environment can be one of the most challenging aspects of obedience and behavior training. Public spaces like busy streets, parks, markets, festivals, and events are filled with distractions—people, loud noises, unfamiliar scents, and unexpected movements—that can overwhelm a dog. However, with the right techniques, patience, and gradual exposure, dogs can learn to stay focused and obedient even in the most chaotic environments.

Successfully training in such settings requires careful preparation, confidence-building exercises, and a structured approach to desensitization.

Why Training in Crowded and Noisy Environments is Important

Training in high-distraction areas is beneficial for both dogs and their handlers. Some key reasons include:

- Building Confidence: Dogs that are exposed to different sounds, people, and environments from an early age become more adaptable and less fearful.
- Enhancing Focus and Obedience: Practicing commands in distracting situations reinforces a dog's ability to listen and respond reliably.
- Reducing Anxiety and Reactivity: Gradual exposure helps prevent excessive fear or aggression toward new sights, sounds, and people.
- Improving Socialization Skills: Proper training in public ensures that dogs behave appropriately around other dogs, people, and unexpected situations.
- Preparing for Real-Life Scenarios: Whether walking through a city, traveling, or visiting pet-friendly establishments, a well-trained dog is easier to manage.

Challenges of Training in Crowded or Noisy Environments

Before beginning training in such settings, it's important to understand the difficulties that dogs may face:

Distractions

- Moving people, other animals, traffic, and food smells can easily break a dog's concentration.
- Sudden loud noises like car horns, sirens, and fireworks can startle an unprepared dog.

Overstimulation and Stress

- Too much sensory input can overwhelm dogs, making them anxious or hyperactive.
- Some dogs may react by pulling on the leash, barking, or refusing to move.

Fear or Reactivity

- Unfamiliar environments may trigger defensive behaviors such as growling or attempting to flee.
- Dogs that are not properly socialized may become aggressive or excessively shy.

Safety Risks

- Crowded areas pose the danger of a dog running away, getting stepped on, or ingesting something harmful.
- Training in busy areas requires heightened awareness to keep the dog safe.

How to Prepare for Training in Crowded or Noisy Environments

Start with Low-Distraction Areas

- Begin training in quiet spaces and gradually introduce mild distractions.
- Use familiar environments before progressing to unpredictable settings.
- Short sessions in slightly challenging areas help build a dog's tolerance over time.

Use High-Value Rewards

- In distracting situations, normal treats may not hold a dog's attention.
- Use especially desirable treats like cooked chicken, cheese, or freeze-dried meat.
- Praise, petting, and engaging toys can also reinforce positive behavior.

Ensure Basic Obedience is Strong

- Dogs should already understand commands like sit, stay, come, leave it, and focus before training in public spaces.
- Strengthening these commands at home makes it easier for dogs to obey in high-stimulation settings.

Choose the Right Equipment

- A well-fitted harness or head collar provides better control than a standard collar.
- A shorter leash (4-6 feet) helps maintain closer control.
- If a dog is prone to reacting, a basket muzzle can prevent unwanted interactions while training.

Practice Calming Techniques

- Teaching settle or watch me commands can help redirect focus when overstimulated.
- Slow breathing exercises and deep-pressure therapy (such as a gentle touch on the chest) can help ease anxiety.

Training Techniques for Success in Busy or Noisy Environments

Gradual Desensitization

- Step 1: Start by exposing the dog to moderate background noise at a distance, such as a park with light foot traffic.
- Step 2: Gradually move closer to more populated areas while monitoring the dog's comfort level.
- Step 3: Increase the intensity by introducing the dog to busier streets, stores, or dog-friendly events.

Focus and Engagement Training

- Teach a "look at me" cue to encourage eye contact despite distractions.
- Reward voluntary check-ins when the dog looks back at the handler.
- Use pattern games, like rewarding every few steps during a loose-leash walk, to keep attention on the handler.

The Power of Distance

- If a dog appears overwhelmed, move to a quieter spot before continuing training.
- Work at a distance where the dog can observe distractions without becoming anxious.
- Slowly decrease distance over multiple training sessions.

Reinforcing Calm Behavior

- Reward a dog for calm reactions to noises, people, and movement.
- Practice sit or down stays in public spaces to reinforce patience.
- If a dog gets overly excited, pause the session and resume only when they are calmer.

Using Environmental Rewards

- Instead of only using food, let the dog explore as a reward for calm behavior.
- If a dog remains focused, allow them to sniff a tree, greet a friendly passerby, or briefly observe an interesting sight.

Redirecting Unwanted Reactions

- If a dog starts barking, lunging, or pulling, use a distraction cue like "let's go" to move in another direction.
- Provide a command to refocus attention, such as "touch" (hand target) or "leave it."
- If reactivity is severe, practice at a greater distance before attempting closer interactions.

Common Training Scenarios and Solutions

Training in a Busy Park

- Begin in a quieter section before moving closer to groups of people.
- Reward the dog for staying close and not pulling toward distractions.
- Gradually increase exposure to joggers, cyclists, and other dogs.

Walking on a Crowded Street

- Train heel walking to prevent excessive pulling.
- Use treats frequently to reinforce focus.
- Stop occasionally to allow the dog to reset and avoid overstimulation.

Handling Loud Noises (Sirens, Fireworks, or Construction Sounds)

- Expose the dog to recorded loud sounds at a low volume and gradually increase.
- Reward calm behavior when exposed to real-life noises.
- Use calming commands like "settle" to reassure the dog.

Navigating a Pet-Friendly Event or Market

- Start with short visits and increase duration over time.
- Keep interactions with strangers and other dogs controlled and positive.
- Watch body language to ensure the dog remains comfortable.

Troubleshooting Issues in Noisy or Crowded Training Sessions

Dog Becomes Overwhelmed or Fearful

- Move to a quieter location and let the dog observe from a safe distance.
- Offer calming cues like slow petting or a chew toy.

Dog Pulls Excessively on the Leash

- Use a front-clip harness to reduce pulling force.
- Stop walking whenever the dog pulls, rewarding loose-leash walking.

Dog Jumps on Strangers in Excitement

- Teach a solid "sit for greetings" routine.
- Instruct strangers to ignore the dog until it remains calm.

Dog is Distracted and Ignores Commands

- Increase the value of rewards in high-distraction areas.
- Train at lower-distraction levels before progressing to more difficult settings.

Training in crowded or noisy environments takes patience and consistency, but it is a vital skill for any dog.

Safety Considerations for Outdoor Adventures

Exploring the outdoors with your dog can be a rewarding and enriching experience. Whether you are hiking through the mountains, camping in the wilderness, taking a stroll in the park, or enjoying a day at the beach, outdoor adventures provide excellent opportunities for exercise, bonding, and mental stimulation. However, safety should always be a top priority to ensure both you and your dog enjoy the adventure without unnecessary risks.

From wildlife encounters to extreme weather conditions and hazardous terrain, outdoor environments present numerous challenges that require preparation and awareness. Understanding these risks and taking the right precautions can prevent accidents, injuries, and stress while making the experience enjoyable for both you and your furry companion.

Pre-Adventure Preparation: Setting the Stage for a Safe Outing

Know Your Destination

Before heading out, research your chosen outdoor location. Some trails, parks, and beaches may have restrictions regarding dogs, specific leash laws, or potential hazards. Consider the following:

- Dog-Friendly Policies: Not all hiking trails, campsites, or beaches allow dogs. Ensure the location welcomes dogs before heading out.
- Leash Requirements: Some areas may require dogs to be leashed at all times, while others offer off-leash sections.
- Wildlife Presence: Research whether dangerous animals like bears, coyotes, snakes, or poisonous plants are common in the area.
- Weather Conditions: Check the forecast to avoid extreme heat, cold, storms, or sudden weather changes that could put your dog at risk.

Physical Conditioning and Health Check

Dogs need to be physically prepared for outdoor activities, especially strenuous hikes or long adventures. Before venturing out:

- Vet Check-Up: Ensure your dog is up to date on vaccinations, flea and tick prevention, and is in good overall health.
- Fitness Assessment: Senior dogs, puppies, or dogs with medical conditions may require shorter, less strenuous adventures.
- Paw Protection: Rough terrain, hot pavement, or cold snow can injure your dog's paws. Consider using protective booties or paw wax.
- Hydration and Nutrition: Bring enough food and water for both you and your dog to prevent dehydration and exhaustion.

Essential Gear for Outdoor Safety

Leash and Collar/Harness

A sturdy leash and a well-fitted collar or harness are essential for maintaining control in unpredictable environments.

- Retractable leashes can be dangerous in areas with heavy foliage or steep terrain. A standard 4-6 ft leash is safer.
- Reflective gear or LED collars improve visibility during early morning or evening adventures.
- Harnesses provide better control, especially for dogs prone to pulling.

ID Tags and Microchips

In case your dog gets lost, proper identification can help ensure a safe return.

- Up-to-date ID tags with your contact information and address are crucial.
- Microchipping provides an added layer of security in case the collar or tags fall off.
- GPS trackers can be attached to collars for added peace of mind.

First Aid Kit for Dogs

A canine first aid kit can be a lifesaver in case of injuries or emergencies. Items to include:

- Antiseptic wipes and antibiotic ointment
- Bandages and gauze
- Tweezers (for tick or thorn removal)
- Hydrogen peroxide (to induce vomiting if needed under vet guidance)
- Emergency vet contact information

Water and Travel Bowls

Dogs can easily become dehydrated, especially in hot or dry conditions. Always carry:

- A collapsible water bowl for easy drinking access.
- Plenty of fresh water (avoid letting your dog drink from stagnant water sources, which may carry bacteria or parasites).

Protective Clothing (If Needed)

Depending on the weather conditions, your dog may need extra protection:

- Cooling vests for hot climates to prevent overheating.
- Insulated jackets for cold or snowy environments.
- Booties to protect paws from hot pavement, sharp rocks, or icy surfaces.

On-the-Trail Safety Tips

Leash Control and Recall Training

Even if the area allows off-leash dogs, maintaining control is crucial for safety.

- Use a long leash for added freedom while maintaining control.
- Train a strong recall command (like "Come!" or a whistle) to ensure your dog returns immediately if called.

Avoiding Hazards on the Trail

- Wildlife Encounters: Keep your dog away from wild animals, even if they seem harmless.
- Poisonous Plants and Mushrooms: Many plants, such as poison ivy, oleander, or wild mushrooms, can be toxic to dogs.
- Steep Drops and Cliff Edges: Keep dogs away from dangerous falls.

Dealing with Unfamiliar Dogs and People

- Always assess an approaching dog before allowing interaction.
- If an off-leash dog approaches, stand between your dog and the other dog if necessary.
- Not everyone is comfortable with dogs; keep your dog from jumping or lunging at people.

Water Safety for Lakes, Rivers, and Beaches

Swimming Safety

Not all dogs are natural swimmers, and even strong swimmers can struggle in strong currents.

- Use a dog life jacket for added buoyancy and visibility.

- Introduce your dog gradually to water if they are inexperienced swimmers.
- Watch for waterborne hazards, including sharp rocks, strong tides, or contaminated water.

Preventing Waterborne Illnesses

- Avoid stagnant water that may contain bacteria, parasites, or blue-green algae, which can be fatal if ingested.
- Rinse your dog after swimming to remove sand, salt, or bacteria.

Weather-Related Safety Considerations

Hot Weather and Heatstroke Prevention

- Avoid hiking during peak sun hours (late morning to early afternoon).
- Provide plenty of shade breaks and fresh water.
- Signs of heatstroke include excessive panting, drooling, lethargy, and vomiting. If suspected, move to a shaded area, offer water, and seek veterinary help immediately.

Cold Weather Precautions

- Short-haired and small dogs may need insulated coats in freezing temperatures.
- Snow can cause frostbite on paws, so paw wax or booties can help.
- Avoid frozen lakes—thin ice can be dangerous.

Camping with Your Dog: Overnight Safety Considerations

Sleeping Arrangements

- Bring a dog bed or blanket to keep your dog comfortable and warm.
- Keep your dog inside the tent at night to prevent encounters with wildlife.

Fire Safety

- Keep dogs away from campfires, grills, and cooking stoves.
- Store food securely to avoid attracting wildlife.

Protecting Against Insects and Parasites

- Apply flea and tick preventatives before outdoor adventures.
- Check for ticks after the outing, paying attention to the ears, belly, and paws.
- Avoid areas heavily populated with mosquitoes, which can transmit heartworm disease.

Emergency Situations: What to Do

Lost Dog Protocol

If your dog gets lost:

1. Stay calm and call your dog's name.
2. Return to your last known location where your dog may try to find you.
3. Notify local authorities or park rangers if in a national park or public area.

Injury or Medical Emergency

- For cuts or wounds, clean the injury with antiseptic and bandage it.
- If your dog suffers a snake bite or heatstroke, get veterinary help immediately.
- Carry your dog out of the area if they are unable to walk.

Outdoor adventures with your dog can be incredible experiences filled with fun, exercise, and bonding. However, preparation and awareness are key to ensuring safety in different environments. By equipping yourself with the right knowledge, gear, and emergency preparedness, you can enjoy stress-free, memorable outings with your furry companion while keeping them safe, comfortable, and happy.

Chapter 12: Maintaining Good Behavior for Life

Training is not a one-time event but a lifelong journey. To ensure lasting good behavior, consistency, reinforcement, and adaptability are essential. This chapter explores strategies to maintain discipline, prevent regression, and strengthen the bond between you and your dog.

Reinforcing Training Over Time

Training a dog is not just about teaching basic commands or solving immediate behavioral issues—it's about maintaining and reinforcing good behavior throughout your dog's life. Without ongoing reinforcement, even the most well-trained dogs can gradually forget or ignore commands, leading to behavioral regression. Ensuring your dog continues to follow commands, behaves well in various situations, and stays mentally engaged requires consistency, patience, and a commitment to lifelong learning.

Reinforcement training isn't about constant drilling or strict discipline; rather, it's about naturally incorporating training into your dog's daily routine, adapting to their needs as they grow, and keeping the experience enjoyable for both of you. Whether you have a puppy, an adult dog, or a senior canine, reinforcing training over time will strengthen your bond and keep your dog well-behaved for life.

The Importance of Ongoing Reinforcement

Dogs, like humans, can forget skills if they are not regularly practiced. Without reinforcement, commands can lose their effectiveness, and previously well-established behaviors may deteriorate. Regular reinforcement helps:

- Strengthen long-term memory: By revisiting training periodically, your dog retains learned behaviors.
- Prevent behavioral regression: Without practice, your dog may begin testing boundaries or ignoring commands.
- Improve adaptability: As your dog ages, encounters new situations, or experiences life changes, reinforcing training ensures they remain well-behaved in different contexts.
- Strengthen your bond: Positive reinforcement training strengthens trust and communication between you and your dog.

Daily Practices to Reinforce Training

Consistency in Commands and Expectations

One of the most effective ways to reinforce training is to maintain consistency in the commands you use and the expectations you set.

- Use the same words and hand signals for each command to avoid confusion.
- Ensure everyone in the household follows the same training rules to prevent mixed messages.
- Avoid allowing bad behaviors "just this once"—this can undo months of training.

Incorporating Training into Everyday Life

Rather than setting aside separate training sessions, integrate commands into daily activities.

- Ask your dog to "sit" before meals instead of just giving them food.
- Use "stay" before opening the door to prevent door-dashing.
- Reinforce recall by calling your dog to you randomly throughout the day and rewarding them.
- Have your dog practice "leave it" during walks when encountering distractions.

Reinforce Good Behavior with Rewards

Dogs thrive on positive reinforcement. Even after they've mastered a command, occasional rewards keep them motivated.

- Continue using treats, praise, or playtime as occasional reinforcement.
- Reduce treats gradually but continue verbal praise and affection.
- Rotate different rewards to keep your dog engaged.

Practicing Commands in Different Environments

Dogs often associate commands with specific places, meaning they may obey at home but struggle in new environments.

- Practice commands in varied locations, such as parks, busy streets, and pet-friendly stores.
- Introduce new distractions gradually, reinforcing focus and obedience.
- Encourage training in real-life situations, such as having your dog sit calmly during vet visits or at outdoor cafes.

Advanced Reinforcement Techniques

Proofing Commands Against Distractions

Even a well-trained dog may struggle to listen when faced with distractions.

- Increase distractions gradually while reinforcing obedience.

- Use the three D's of proofing:
    - Distance (Command your dog from farther away)
    - Duration (Have your dog hold a command for longer periods)
    - Distractions (Practice in different settings with increasing levels of distractions)

Refreshing Old Commands and Teaching New Ones

Even if your dog knows the basics, revisiting old commands keeps them sharp.

- Periodically test all learned commands to ensure retention.
- Add new commands or fun tricks to keep training exciting.
- Try engaging activities like agility training, nose work, or puzzle games to challenge your dog's mind.

Reinforcing Impulse Control and Patience

Impulse control is a skill that needs constant reinforcement.

- Have your dog wait for permission before eating, playing, or going outside.
- Reward calm behavior instead of excessive excitement.
- Reinforce "leave it" and "wait" commands regularly.

Adapting Reinforcement to Different Life Stages

Puppies and Young Dogs

- Keep sessions short and fun to match their short attention spans.
- Frequently revisit commands to strengthen retention.
- Socialization should continue as they grow to maintain good manners.

Adult Dogs

- Maintain a routine of regular training refreshers.
- Challenge them with new experiences, environments, and commands.
- Prevent bad habits from developing by remaining consistent with rules.

Senior Dogs

- Adjust training based on their physical abilities and limitations.
- Use gentler reinforcement methods and shorter training sessions.
- Focus on mental stimulation to keep their minds sharp.

Preventing Behavioral Regression

Even well-trained dogs can backslide if training is neglected. Here's how to prevent regression:

- Stay proactive: Don't wait for bad behaviors to appear before reinforcing training.
- Catch and correct early: If your dog begins ignoring commands, immediately reinforce training.
- Use occasional refresher sessions: Brief training sessions throughout the week help maintain skills.
- Stay engaged: Training is a lifelong process—keep things fun and challenging for your dog.

Reinforcing training over time is essential for maintaining good behavior, ensuring obedience in different situations, and keeping your dog mentally stimulated.

How to Keep Training Fun and Engaging for Your Dog

Training your dog should be a rewarding experience for both you and your furry companion. However, many pet owners struggle with keeping their dog's attention, maintaining enthusiasm, and ensuring that training remains a positive experience rather than a chore. If training sessions become dull or repetitive, your dog may lose interest, making progress slow and frustrating.

To keep training enjoyable and engaging, you need to implement a mix of creativity, patience, and positive reinforcement techniques. Here's how you can make training fun, effective, and something your dog looks forward to.

Use Positive Reinforcement

Dogs learn best when they associate training with positive experiences. Positive reinforcement training involves rewarding your dog for good behavior rather than punishing mistakes. This creates a strong bond of trust and motivation for your dog to participate in training sessions willingly.

How to Implement Positive Reinforcement

- Use high-value treats that your dog loves the most, such as small pieces of chicken or cheese.
- Praise and affection can be just as effective as food rewards, so use verbal praise like "Good job!" combined with petting and belly rubs.
- Play as a reward by incorporating fetch or tug-of-war as a way to reinforce good behavior.

When your dog realizes that training leads to rewards, they will be excited to participate and eager to learn more.

Keep Sessions Short and Exciting

Dogs, especially puppies, have short attention spans. Training for too long can lead to frustration and boredom. To maintain enthusiasm, keep sessions brief and effective. If you notice your dog losing interest, take a break and return later. Always end on a positive note by asking your dog to do something they already know and rewarding them for it.

Short, frequent training sessions are more effective than long, drawn-out ones.

Incorporate Play into Training

Dogs love to play, and using games in training keeps them engaged. Instead of strict, repetitive drills, integrate fun activities such as:

- Hide and seek by calling your dog's name from another room and rewarding them when they find you.
- Fetch training where you teach commands like "drop it" or "bring it back."
- Obstacle courses using household items like chairs and tunnels to encourage agility.
- Find the treat by hiding treats around a room and letting your dog search for them.

Play-based training not only enhances learning but also strengthens your bond with your dog.

Rotate Training Environments

Dogs can become bored if they always train in the same spot. To keep training fresh, try different rooms in your home, train in the backyard, or practice commands in a park. This also helps your dog generalize commands, ensuring they respond no matter where they are.

Introduce New Tricks and Challenges

Once your dog masters basic commands, keep their minds engaged by teaching advanced tricks like spinning in a circle, playing dead, rolling over, putting toys away, or weaving through your legs. Learning new tricks prevents boredom and gives your dog a mental workout, keeping training enjoyable.

Use a Variety of Rewards

Dogs can get tired of the same reward over time. Keep things exciting by varying their rewards. Rotate between different treats, use a mix of praise, belly rubs, and toys, and occasionally surprise your dog with a bigger reward like a long play session or a new toy. This keeps your dog motivated and curious about what they'll get next.

Train with Friends and Family

Training doesn't have to be a solo activity. Involve other family members or invite a friend with a dog to join in. This helps your dog learn to obey commands even with distractions. Group training sessions can also introduce socialization opportunities, helping your dog learn good manners around other people and pets.

Add Exciting Challenges

Once your dog understands basic commands, challenge them with distractions. Ask them to "stay" while you leave the room, try training in a busy park, or teach impulse control by placing a treat on the floor and making them wait before eating it. Increasing difficulty keeps training stimulating and fun.

Keep a Positive Attitude

Dogs are highly perceptive to human emotions. If you're frustrated or bored, your dog will pick up on it. Always keep a positive tone, smile, and make training enjoyable. If you feel frustrated, take a break and try again later with renewed energy.

Allow for Free Play and Breaks

Training shouldn't feel like work for your dog. Allow time for free play where they can just be a dog. This helps prevent burnout and keeps them eager for the next training session.

Be Patient and Celebrate Small Wins

Training takes time, and each dog learns at their own pace. Celebrate small victories, whether it's a simple "sit" or a complicated trick. This encourages your dog to keep trying and enjoy the learning process.

Mix Old and New Commands

To prevent boredom, mix up training by practicing both old and new commands. This reinforces what they've learned while keeping sessions engaging. If you're teaching "stay," mix in commands like "shake" or "sit" to keep things unpredictable.

Training should be an enjoyable and rewarding experience for both you and your dog.

Common Mistakes Owners Make and How to Avoid Them

Being a pet owner is a rewarding experience, but it also comes with responsibilities. Many dog owners, whether new or experienced, unintentionally make mistakes that can affect their pet's behavior, health, and overall well-being. While these mistakes are often made with good intentions, they can lead to behavioral issues, stress, or even health problems for your dog. Understanding these common mistakes and knowing how to avoid them can help you become a better pet parent and build a stronger, happier bond with your dog.

Inconsistent Training

Dogs thrive on routine and consistency. One of the biggest mistakes owners make is being inconsistent with training. This can confuse your dog and make it difficult for them to understand what is expected.

How to Avoid It

- Establish clear rules from the beginning and ensure everyone in the household follows them.
- Use the same commands and reinforcement techniques to avoid confusion.
- Practice commands regularly, even after your dog has learned them, to maintain obedience.

Lack of Socialization

Socialization is crucial for a dog's development. Many owners fail to expose their dogs to different people, environments, and other animals during their critical early months, which can result in fearfulness, anxiety, or aggression.

How to Avoid It

- Expose your dog to various environments, sounds, and experiences in a positive way.
- Introduce them to friendly dogs and people from an early age.
- Reward calm and confident behavior during socialization experiences.

Punishing Instead of Rewarding

Many owners resort to punishment when their dog misbehaves, believing it will stop unwanted behavior. However, punishment can lead to fear, anxiety, and even aggression.

How to Avoid It

- Focus on positive reinforcement by rewarding good behavior with treats, praise, or toys.
- Redirect unwanted behavior instead of punishing it. For example, if your dog chews on furniture, give them an appropriate chew toy instead.
- Be patient and consistent in reinforcing good habits.

Overfeeding or Feeding the Wrong Diet

Many owners unintentionally overfeed their dogs or give them food that is unhealthy or inappropriate. This can lead to obesity, digestive problems, and other health issues.

How to Avoid It

- Feed your dog a balanced diet suited to their breed, age, and activity level.

- Avoid giving table scraps or foods that are toxic to dogs, such as chocolate, onions, and grapes.
- Follow portion guidelines and measure food to prevent overfeeding.

Neglecting Exercise Needs

Some owners underestimate their dog's need for physical activity. A lack of exercise can lead to obesity, hyperactivity, and destructive behavior.

How to Avoid It

- Ensure your dog gets daily exercise based on their breed and energy level.
- Engage in activities like walks, runs, fetch, and agility training.
- Provide mental stimulation through puzzle toys, training sessions, and interactive games.

Ignoring Dental Health

Dental care is often overlooked, but poor oral hygiene can lead to gum disease, tooth loss, and other health problems.

How to Avoid It

- Brush your dog's teeth regularly with dog-safe toothpaste.
- Provide dental chews or toys designed to reduce plaque buildup.
- Schedule regular veterinary dental check-ups.

Not Providing Enough Mental Stimulation

Many owners focus on physical exercise but forget about mental stimulation. Dogs need to use their brains to stay happy and engaged.

How to Avoid It

- Teach your dog new tricks and commands.
- Use puzzle toys and treat-dispensing games.
- Rotate toys to keep their interest and prevent boredom.

Allowing Bad Behavior to Go Unchecked

Some owners ignore small behavioral issues, thinking they will resolve on their own. Unfortunately, minor problems can escalate into serious behavioral issues over time.

How to Avoid It

- Address unwanted behaviors immediately with positive reinforcement and redirection.
- Be consistent in correcting behaviors like jumping, barking excessively, or pulling on the leash.
- Seek professional help from a trainer or behaviorist if needed.

Skipping Routine Vet Visits

Some owners only take their dog to the vet when there's a visible health issue, but regular check-ups are essential for early detection of problems.

How to Avoid It

- Schedule annual vet visits for check-ups and vaccinations.
- Monitor your dog for any changes in appetite, energy levels, or behavior.
- Keep up with preventative care, including flea, tick, and heartworm treatments.

Using the Wrong Collar or Harness

Improper use of collars and harnesses can cause discomfort, injuries, or ineffective leash training.

How to Avoid It

- Choose a well-fitting collar or harness suitable for your dog's size and breed.
- Avoid using prong or choke collars, as they can cause harm and lead to fear-based behavior.
- Train your dog to walk on a loose leash rather than relying on corrective tools.

Leaving a Dog Alone for Too Long

Dogs are social animals, and prolonged isolation can lead to anxiety, depression, and destructive behavior.

How to Avoid It

- Spend quality time with your dog through play, training, and bonding activities.
- If you're away for long hours, arrange for a pet sitter, dog walker, or dog daycare.
- Provide enrichment toys and activities to keep them occupied when alone.

Failing to Provide a Safe Environment

Some owners overlook potential dangers in their home that can pose risks to their dogs.

How to Avoid It

- Keep toxic foods, household cleaners, and small objects out of reach.
- Ensure your yard is securely fenced to prevent escapes.
- Provide a comfortable space with proper bedding, shade, and fresh water.

Expecting Too Much Too Soon

Many owners get frustrated when their dog doesn't learn a command immediately or struggles with training.

How to Avoid It

- Be patient and understand that learning takes time.
- Use gradual steps and set realistic expectations based on your dog's age and ability.
- Celebrate small successes to keep training positive and enjoyable.

Owning a dog is a big responsibility, and mistakes are bound to happen. However, by being aware of common pitfalls and actively working to avoid them, you can create a positive, loving, and structured environment for your furry friend. Consistency, patience, and a commitment to your dog's well-being will help you build a happy, well-adjusted pet that thrives in your care.

Creating a Customized Training Plan for Your Dog

Training your dog is an essential part of pet ownership, ensuring they develop good manners, listen to commands, and become well-behaved members of your family. However, no two dogs are the same. Breed, age, temperament, and previous experiences all play a role in how a dog learns. This is why a one-size-fits-all approach to training doesn't work for every dog.

A customized training plan takes your dog's unique needs into account, helping them learn in a way that is effective, enjoyable, and suited to their personality. A well-structured training plan helps set clear expectations, builds a strong bond between you and your dog, and creates a positive learning environment.

Understanding Your Dog's Personality and Needs

Before creating a training plan, take time to assess your dog's unique characteristics. These factors will influence how you train and what methods will be most effective.

Factors to Consider:

- Breed Traits – Some breeds are naturally more energetic, independent, or stubborn, which can affect how they respond to training.

- Age – Puppies learn differently than adult or senior dogs. Younger dogs are more adaptable, while older dogs may need extra patience.
- Temperament – Is your dog shy, confident, excitable, or anxious? Understanding their temperament helps tailor your approach.
- Previous Training or Experiences – A rescue dog with a history of neglect may require a different approach than a dog raised from puppyhood in a stable home.
- Energy Levels – High-energy breeds need more physical and mental stimulation during training to stay engaged.

Setting Clear Training Goals

A customized training plan should outline what you want to achieve with your dog. Setting clear goals helps track progress and keeps training focused.

Common Training Goals:

- Teaching basic commands like sit, stay, come, down, and leave it
- House training and potty training
- Leash manners and loose leash walking
- Socialization with people and other dogs
- Preventing bad habits like jumping, excessive barking, or digging
- Advanced training such as off-leash recall, agility, or trick training

Prioritize the most important goals based on your dog's needs. For example, a new puppy may need focus on potty training and basic commands, while an older dog may require leash training or behavior modification.

Choosing the Right Training Methods

Dogs learn best through positive reinforcement, which involves rewarding good behavior rather than punishing mistakes. The key is to find what motivates your dog.

Reward-Based Training

- Food Rewards – Small, tasty treats work well for most dogs. Use high-value treats for difficult tasks.
- Praise and Affection – Some dogs respond better to verbal praise, belly rubs, or a happy tone of voice.
- Toys and Play – Fetch, tug-of-war, or a favorite toy can be a great reward.

Avoid harsh corrections, yelling, or punishment-based training, as these can create fear and confusion, leading to behavioral issues.

Structuring a Training Routine

Consistency is crucial when training your dog. A structured plan helps reinforce learning and makes training sessions effective.

Training Session Guidelines:

- Keep Sessions Short and Frequent – Dogs learn best in short bursts, so aim for 5-15 minute sessions multiple times a day.
- Train in Different Environments – Practice commands at home, in the backyard, and in public places to help your dog generalize skills.
- Use Everyday Situations for Training – Incorporate training into daily activities, such as asking your dog to "sit" before meals or "stay" before opening the door.
- Always End on a Positive Note – Finish each session with an easy command your dog knows well and reward them for success.

Building a Step-by-Step Training Plan

A training plan should progress in stages, from basic skills to more advanced behaviors.

Step 1: Foundation Training

Start with basic obedience and essential life skills.

- Teach your dog their name and establish a strong "come" command.
- Introduce sit, stay, and down using treats and praise.
- Begin house training and create a consistent potty schedule.
- Teach leash manners to prevent pulling and frustration on walks.

Step 2: Socialization and Exposure

- Expose your dog to new sounds, sights, and experiences to prevent fear and anxiety.
- Arrange positive meetings with other dogs and people.
- Get your dog comfortable with grooming, vet visits, and handling.

Step 3: Intermediate Training

Once your dog masters the basics, introduce more complex commands.

- Teach leave it, drop it, and wait to improve impulse control.
- Work on recall (come when called) in distracting environments.
- Train settle and calm behaviors for relaxation.

Step 4: Advanced Training and Problem Solving

- Strengthen off-leash reliability with long-distance recall training.
- Practice training around high distractions such as busy parks or dog-friendly cafes.
- Address problem behaviors like jumping, barking, or separation anxiety.
- Explore fun activities like agility, scent work, or trick training to keep learning exciting.

Adjusting the Plan Based on Progress

Not all dogs learn at the same pace, so adjust your plan as needed. If your dog struggles with a command, break it down into smaller steps and go at their pace. Be flexible and patient.

Signs to Adjust Training:

- Your dog seems confused or frustrated – simplify the lesson.
- Training has become too easy – increase difficulty with distractions.
- Progress has stalled – try a new reward or training method.

Tracking Your Dog's Progress

Keeping a training journal can help you track improvements and identify areas needing more practice.

What to Track:

- Commands learned and progress made
- Challenges or setbacks encountered
- Reward types that work best
- Improvements in behavior over time

Overcoming Common Training Challenges

Training isn't always smooth, and owners may face obstacles along the way.

Common Problems and Solutions:

- Short Attention Span – Use high-value treats and make training sessions fun.
- Lack of Motivation – Switch up rewards or try training before meals when your dog is hungry.
- Ignoring Commands – Go back to basics and reinforce commands in a distraction-free environment.
- Fear or Anxiety – Move at a slow, comfortable pace and create positive experiences.

Creating a customized training plan ensures your dog learns at their own pace while making training enjoyable and effective. By setting clear goals, using positive reinforcement, and adapting to your dog's individual needs, you can create a training program that fosters obedience, confidence, and a happy relationship between you and your dog.

Training is a lifelong journey, and with patience, consistency, and the right approach, you'll have a well-mannered and happy dog eager to learn and please.

Final Thoughts

Training and caring for a dog is a journey filled with learning, patience, and deep companionship. Whether you are welcoming a new puppy into your home or working with an older dog, the time and effort you invest in their training and well-being will shape their behavior, confidence, and happiness. A well-trained dog is not just obedient; they are a secure, well-adjusted companion who understands the world around them, trusts their owner, and thrives in a structured and loving environment.

One of the most important lessons in dog training is that it is a lifelong commitment. Dogs never stop learning, and their training should never be seen as a task with a final destination. Instead, it is an evolving process that strengthens the bond between you and your dog. Every interaction you have with them is an opportunity to reinforce positive behaviors, build trust, and ensure they feel safe, loved, and understood.

The Power of Positive Reinforcement

Modern training techniques emphasize positive reinforcement, which is rooted in trust, encouragement, and understanding. The days of harsh punishment and outdated training methods are behind us. Science and experience have shown that dogs learn best when they feel safe and rewarded. By using positive reinforcement, you foster an environment where learning is fun and rewarding, rather than stressful and fear-driven.

When you reward desired behaviors, your dog will naturally want to repeat them. When you set clear expectations and communicate effectively, your dog will develop confidence and trust in you. Training should always be a conversation, never a confrontation.

Patience and Consistency: The Key to Success

Training is not always easy. There will be moments of frustration, setbacks, and challenges. But through patience and consistency, you will see progress. Dogs do not learn overnight, and some may take longer than others to grasp certain commands or behaviors. Each dog learns at their own pace, and it is crucial to celebrate even the smallest victories.

Consistency in your commands, expectations, and rewards will reinforce learning. If you allow certain behaviors one day and correct them the next, your dog will become confused. Clear communication, unwavering patience, and a steady routine will lead to long-term success.

Strengthening the Bond Between You and Your Dog

Training is about more than just obedience—it is about building a deep, meaningful relationship with your dog. The process of training fosters mutual respect, understanding, and trust. A dog that feels understood and valued will be more eager to listen, learn, and please their owner.

By spending time together in training sessions, playtime, and daily interactions, you create a connection that goes beyond simple commands. Dogs are incredibly intuitive creatures, and they respond to love, patience, and encouragement. When they know they can trust you, they will look to you for guidance, making training more natural and enjoyable.

Adapting to Your Dog's Unique Needs

No two dogs are the same, and a training method that works perfectly for one dog may not work for another. Understanding your dog's unique personality, energy levels, and learning style will help you customize their training to suit them best.

Some dogs are naturally independent and require more motivation, while others are eager to please and will quickly pick up new skills. Some are shy and need gentle encouragement, while others are confident and require structured guidance. By adapting your training approach to fit your dog's personality, you create an environment where they can thrive.

Lifelong Learning and Growth

Training does not stop after your dog masters basic commands. There is always room for growth, enrichment, and new challenges. Teaching advanced commands, fun tricks, or engaging in specialized training like agility or scent work keeps your dog mentally and physically stimulated.

Continued training also helps prevent boredom, which can lead to destructive behaviors. Dogs, like humans, need purpose and engagement in their daily lives. Regular training sessions, interactive play, and structured activities will keep them happy, balanced, and well-behaved.

Overcoming Challenges with Patience and Love

Every dog owner will encounter challenges. Whether it is house training accidents, leash pulling, excessive barking, or separation anxiety, no dog is perfect. The key to overcoming these challenges is to approach them with patience, understanding, and a problem-solving mindset.

Dogs are not deliberately difficult; they simply communicate in their own way. If a problem arises, take a step back and analyze the situation. Is your dog trying to tell you something? Are they scared, confused, or overstimulated? Addressing the root cause of a behavior is far more effective than simply trying to suppress it.

Mistakes will happen, and that is okay. What matters most is how you respond. Correct behavior with kindness, guide your dog with confidence, and always reinforce positive actions.

The Joy of a Well-Trained Dog

A well-trained dog is a joy to live with. They can accompany you on adventures, interact politely with guests, walk calmly by your side, and understand what is expected of them in different situations. They become not just pets, but cherished companions who bring happiness, loyalty, and unconditional love.

The time, effort, and patience you invest in training will reward you with a dog that is confident, happy, and well-adjusted. The bond you share with them will be one of trust, respect, and deep companionship.

Final Words: A Journey of Love and Commitment

As you embark on or continue your training journey with your dog, remember that every step, every challenge, and every success strengthens your relationship. Dogs do not ask for much—just love, guidance, and consistency. They look to us for leadership, security, and companionship.

By dedicating yourself to their training, understanding their needs, and providing a structured yet loving environment, you are giving them the best life possible. They, in turn, will give you their loyalty, love, and devotion for a lifetime.

Training is not just about teaching commands—it is about creating a bond that lasts forever. Enjoy the journey, celebrate the milestones, and cherish the incredible relationship you build with your dog.

Printed in Great Britain
by Amazon